The Jesus Way

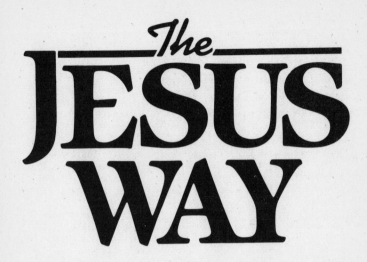

The JESUS WAY

JEAN HOWARD POE

BROADMAN PRESS
Nashville, Tennessee

© Copyright 1988 ● Broadman Press

All Rights Reserved

4250-61

ISBN: 0-8054-5061-0

Dewey Decimal Classification: 232

Subject Heading: JESUS CHRIST // CHRISTIAN LIFE

Library of Congress Catalog Number: 87-33856

Printed in the United States of America

Library of Congress Cataloging-in-Publication Data

Poe, Jean Howard, 1926-
  The Jesus way.

  1. Jesus Christ—Person and offices.   2. Christian
life—Baptist authors.   I. Title.
BT202.P575   1988   232.9'04   87-33856
ISBN 0-8054-5061-0

To my husband, John,
who is a source of
encouragement and sweetness

Contents

Introduction

Problems! Everybody has them. There are problems that aggravate and irritate. There are more serious problems that strip the soul and leave one sitting in the dust. What kind of problems do you have?

Family differences?
Personality conflicts?
Peer pressure?
Loneliness?
Employer-employee frictions?
Too much responsibility?
Lack of the necessities of life?

Did you ever stop to think that Jesus also had His share of problems? The reason we can take our problems to Jesus is because He faced them all. He knows what they do to us and what we can do with them. God's Word tells us that He suffered in *all* ways, being tempted like we are, yet without sin. Jesus with problems? Oh, yes! But He had special immunity from the hurt, the slights, the pettinesses, the major problems that we have to suffer. Right? Wrong!

Leading a perfect life did not protect Jesus from problems and temptations. His perfect life came not only as a result of His nature, but as a *result of* facing and overcoming *without* giving in or falling victim to the problems that attacked Him.

Problems assail all people, whether they are good or bad, holy or

9

profane, right or wrong, young or old. There is no exemption from problems. We need to examine specific problems Jesus faced and learn how He overcame temptations and dilemmas, and we need to know His methods for overcoming. Even though Jesus lived under continuous pressure and attack, He spoke often of "my joy," "life abundantly", "peace," and "happy are you." In spite of His trials and tribulations He had found the secret of true serenity and joy.

See if you can find *your* basic problems among the many mentioned in this book. This is by no means an exhaustive search of all the problems Jesus faced, but perhaps you will find truths that will help you understand your role in your problems and how Jesus would have resolved similar problems. Hopefully, you will find a greater faith in Jesus Christ and His power to understand your situation and His willingness to help you toward a solution.

I have used the words *temptations* and *problem* interchangeably. Jesus was tempted through the problems He faced. Temptations present us with problems, and problems provide and provoke temptations.

After almost two thousand years, it has become difficult for us to think of Jesus as a real person. In our minds we have "protected" Him from hurt, problems, filth, physical necessities, and disappointments. How many times have you imaged Jesus with flesh and bones, dirty clothes, windblown hair or as hungry, thirsty, and tired?

Let's take a look at Jesus' personal life—His personal world. Let's see if we can discover where we have lost contact with His reality as a person—a human being. Let's see what part human emotions and will played in His life. We have tried, and many times succeeded, in divorcing His teachings from His person. We have tried to base our lives only on what He said without giving the necessary attention to *who* He was, what He did, and how He lived.

We, as Christians, often fail to transmit a relevant Christ. Perhaps it is because we, as yet, have not actualized Him for today's world in our own thinking. Now pause for a minute. Don't we picture Jesus as He is portrayed in lovely paintings: healthy, clean-looking hair and beard flowing in the breeze, sparklingly clean children, and clean, well-dressed men and women following in His wake—no worries, no real problems that He could not handle easily—confident, almost self-assured? Or perhaps we may imagine Him seated on a white rock before the multitudes—speaking in quiet tones and His voice carrying to the far ends of the crowd. Then again, we may think of Jesus as a man who, in the face of problems, quickly had a special "line" to God, so He really didn't have to struggle with the solutions and answers to problems. Can you picture Him as frustrated, tired, dirty, disappointed, surprised, and crying real tears with emotion? I am not being profane or sacrilegious.

Did Jesus *really,* honestly have problems? What kind of problems? How did He handle His problems? Since He was God incarnate, was life easier?

If we can understand more clearly Jesus' physical human life, we will be able to appreciate more completely the extent, the immensity, the completeness of His life, death, burial, and resurrection. His own words say:

> "I lay down My life for the sheep . . . I lay it down *on My own initiative.*"[1]

When Jesus spoke these words, He had a very realistic concept of life, suffering, sin, people, and their true nature. These are not the words of a visionary with a dramatic sense of martyrdom but those of a man who had squarely faced the alternatives and had chosen a positive, irreversible direction and purpose.

Therefore, it was not blind idealism that led Him to give His life as a ransom for many. He knew what life was all about. He understood what people really are and what they do. Yet in His immeasurable love, He *chose* to die for us and as many as would believe and receive Him as Savior and Lord.

As we study about Jesus and the problems He faced, please keep an open mind and try to put yourself in the place of Jesus, who put Himself in our place for our salvation. Remember that the trials, temptations, and problems He confronted were all concentrated into thirty-three short years. The majority of the experiences probably fell within the last three years of His life. Our problems and trials cover a long span of years and are tempered with rest and recovery periods. But the great diversity of problems Jesus faced seemed to be crowded into a short span of His life.

Understanding how Jesus approached and dealt with problems can be invaluable to us right now.

> Since therefore the children share in flesh and blood, he himself [Jesus] likewise partook of the same nature, that through death he might destroy him who has the power of death, that is, the devil, and deliver all those who through fear of death were subject to lifelong bondage. For surely it is not with angels that he is concerned but with the descendants of Abraham. Therefore he had to be made like his brethren in every respect, so that he might become a merciful and faithful high priest in the service of God, to make expiation for the sins of the people. For because he himself has suffered and been tempted, he is able to help those who are tempted.[2]

Notes

1. John 10:15, 18 (author's italics)

2. Hebrews 2:14-18, RSV

1

"What Sort of Man Is This?"

Moved with compassion (Mark 1:41).
Tempted in all things (Heb. 4:15).

Jesus, in His perfection, was not above feeling intimately and deeply moved in human situations like those which move and touch modern persons—circumstances which attack the inner being—a person's motives, intentions, attitudes, and methods. In the Book of Hebrews we find these words,

"We have a High Priest who was tempted in every way that we are, but did not sin."[1]

Testing and temptation come to all whether in strong, overt recognizable desires and urges or subtly, almost undetectable impulses. Did you understand the words above? Jesus was tempted (tested) *in every way* that we are! I understand that to mean He faced every kind of problem that attacks and defeats modern persons. He was very much aware—very conscious—of what other people thought, what they said, what they expected—their reactions to Him personally. He was human—God-man.

By the Scriptures we recognize that Jesus was sensitive to the feelings of others. He recognized other people's specific inner needs, as well as their outward needs. In today's world He would be called a gentle man or a gentleman. Jesus' basic method of dealing with the needs of others was to pinpoint in each individual a deep spiritual necessity, as well as a physical one. In Mark's Gospel we have many instances of Jesus' sensitivity to another's need:

1:31—"He came to her and raised her up, *taking her by the hand.*"

1:41—"Moved with compassion, He stretched out His hand and *touched him.*"

5:41—"*Taking the child by the hand.*"

7:33—"*Put His fingers into his ears,* and after spitting, *He touched his tongue* with the saliva."

8:23—"*Taking the blind man by the hand.*

9:27—"But Jesus *took him by the hand* and raised him."

10:16—"He *took them in His arms* and began blessing them, *laying His hands upon them.* (author's italics)

Jesus was the one who made "touch therapy" a part of His everyday life—not as a vulgar, mundane action but one of supreme love and caring.

I would not presume in any way to minimize the Deity of Jesus. He is God, Christ, the Messiah, the Promised One, the Savior of the world, the bright and Morning Star, the Rose of Sharon, the joint Creator of the universe, and my personal, caring Savior. I believe because He is *all* of these and much more. When He came as a baby to this world and grew into manhood here, His human nature was very much a part of Him. He experienced human feelings and struggled with human frailty, human sensations, human testings, trials, and temptations. I feel sure He keenly felt human rejection and ridicule, but *without sin!* The Scriptures tell us that He was tempted in *all* ways like we are.

Do these problems sound familiar to you?

Do you feel rejected?

Do you have to do something that you dread doing?

Do you wonder what people say and think about you?

Do you live under constant pressure?

Do you talk to the same people over and over again without them really understanding what you are saying?

Do you face deep concerns and have *no one* to stand by you for moral support?

Do you face open criticism?

Do you have personal problems?

Do you have too many demands upon your time?

Do you have family problems?

Are you ridiculed and laughed at?

Are you misunderstood by family and friends?

Are you disappointed in someone you love?

Are you required to interrupt your work to take on unrelated tasks?

Have you ever felt unwanted in a particular town or area?

Jesus went through all these human experiences and more. He knew hunger,[2] thirst,[3] and homelessness.[4]

Have you ever thought that we suffer pressures and situations that were not experienced by Jesus and wonder how He can possibly understand? Although the outward circumstances have been altered by our modern mode of life, the basic stresses and inner struggles are the same.

We must not let Jesus' sensitivity be misconstrued to mean weakness or effeminacy. His masculinity cannot be denied, minimized, or questioned. He chose men to be His disciples—men of action, men who were strongly masculine, accustomed to the hard work and responsibilities of a male-oriented world. It was a *man* who made a whip of cords and went through the Temple court driving out the businessmen and religious leaders alike. It was a *man* who overturned the table of the money changers, faced them all, and stated His reason: "Stop making My Father's house a house of merchandise."[5]

It was a *man* who calmly slept in the stern of a boat when hardened, experienced fishermen panicked before the onslaught of a storm.[6] It was a *man* who asked for forgiveness for His tormentors while they were driving spikes through His hands.[7] It was a *man* who was able to withstand forty days and nights without food in a desert place.[8] It was a *man,* who, in the midst of intense suffering, looked down from the cross on a defenseless woman and a helpless young man and made provision for both.[9]

Yet, there never was a man more conscious of the inner needs of those around Him—a sensitivity to the weak and strong, rich and poor, proud and humble, leaders and followers, adults and children, men and women. He was in every respect a gentle man. It might be difficult to believe that He could be so sensitive to the needs and thoughts of others unless He, Himself, had suffered through many harsh and difficult circumstances and experiences.

Jesus did not merely talk about what we do or don't do; He got down to the inner being, the motives, the reasons behind our actions:

> For from within, out of the heart of men, proceed the evil thoughts and fornications, thefts, murders, adulteries, deeds of coveting and wickedness, as well as deceit, sensuality, envy, slander, pride and foolishness. All these evil things proceed from within and defile the man.[10]

Only a sensitive, gentle person who had lived and battled in a real world could recognize and emphasize such a potent philosophy.

Notes

1. Hebrews 4:15, GNB
2. Mark 11:12
3. John 19:28
4. Luke 9:58
5. John 2:13-17
6. Mark 4:35-38
7. Luke 23:33-34
8. Matt. 4:1-2
9. John 19:26-27
10. Mark 7:21-23

2

He Passed the Test

Because he himself was tempted and suffered. (Heb. 2:18a, GNB).
Everything that belongs to the world—what the sinful self desires, what
people see and want, and everything in this world that people are so
proud of (1 John 2:16, GNB).

Jesus went from Nazareth to the Jordan River to be baptized by
John the Baptist. He went with a purpose and sense of mission. The
time had come for Him to seek and to follow the complete will of God
for His life. The first step was to present Himself for public baptism.
He had felt within His heart a stirring and a response to the coaxing
and ministering of the Holy Spirit. When He came up out of the water
after His baptism, the Spirit descended on Him like a dove and a voice
came from heaven, "Thou art My beloved Son, in Thee I am well-
pleased."[1]

After His baptism Jesus was led by the Spirit into the wilderness.
He felt an urgent need to be off to Himself to ponder the workings
and ways of God. He spent forty days without eating, wandering to
and fro, and communing in the Spirit with the Father. Jesus was
initiating a new career—a radical break with the traditional life He
had been living—that of a carpenter supporting His widowed mother
and family. He needed time to line up His priorities, time to comprehend His newly proclaimed status as *Son* of the Heavenly Father—
the Son of God! What did God the Father want Him to do? What were
the implications of the words: "in Thee I am well-pleased." How was
He going to be able to assume the challenge that was before Him?
Although He knew that God had a special place in His life, the
awesome public revelation at His baptism, "Thou art My beloved
Son," meant more than the simple teaching of the Fatherhood of God.

17

This was personal and had a deeper meaning. He needed time to digest the importance of this revelation. Certainly this would change the direction and purpose of His life.

For forty days and nights He kept to the wilderness. Where should He begin? What should be the first step? God's plan coming together in His heart was so different from the popular idea of *how* the Messiah would come and *what* He would do. Jesus meditated as He wandered in the wilderness. He examined the passages of Scripture that He had learned as a youth in the synagogue—the ones that spoke of the Messiah.

The brevity of the biblical account would deceive us into thinking that this was an event of only a few seconds or minutes at the most. Satan waited until Jesus had more or less established His priorities and determined His course, waited until Jesus was physically weakened by hunger. THEN Satan put in his appearance. "If you are the Son,"[2] he began. Did Satan use the same tactics with Jesus that he had used in the Garden of Eden? God had said to Jesus, "Thou art My beloved Son." Satan said, "If You are the Son of God" he then suggested a way to determine if it was true. "You are hungry, no one is around to see You take care of Your own personal needs. After all, IF You are the Son of God, You need to know definitely." It was a hunger as intense as the physical hunger that led Esau to sell his birthright to Jacob when he returned from a hunting trip. Jesus looked at the stones again. What harm could come by changing a few stones into bread? If it really worked, think how much good He could do for the poor and hungry of His own world. Think about the little children who would never have to go to bed hungry again. His own people would not suffer so dreadfully from heavy Roman taxation if they could always have bread to eat.

Jesus' loving Father, through the Holy Spirit, brought to mind the Scriptures from His past learning: "Man shall not live on bread alone." Personal and physical needs and wants are not first priority, no matter how uncomfortable a person feels. Bread is NOT the supreme human need. It is certainly not man's only need. If He relented just this *once,* how could He be sure that the temptation might not return on another occasion? Jesus thought it through and decided His hunger was not so great that it was worth sacrificing His birthright. He remembered the words *You are My beloved Son* that He had heard spoken. He did not need to prove His Sonship—not even to Himself. It was a positive decision. There was no doubt: "Man shall not live on bread alone." His kingdom would definitely *not* be built upon a social order of free handouts of bread; it must be a kingdom of greater purpose and deeper meaning. No, not even for Himself would He use the special powers that had been given Him by a loving, trusting Father.

Soon, after Jesus had determined His position with regard to "what the sinful self desires," He realized that He was in the Holy City on top of the pinnacle of the Temple. He looked down and saw the vast crowds milling around. *He* was their Messiah. He was the one they had been waiting for all their lives. He could comfort and help them. He could fulfill all their needs. This Temple and Jerusalem were to be the center of His work and His reign.

"Now's Your chance," chuckled Satan. "What could be more satisfying to the multitudes than to see their Messiah coming in a spectacular, flamboyant display of power and heavenly protection? Even the Scriptures say He will give His angels[3] commands to lift You up in their hands, so You will not even strike your foot against a stone. Think of the hope and excitement that will surge through the people as they see their Messiah appearing suddenly accompanied by the angels—here at the Temple, God's house!"

Jesus pondered the advisability of such an action. Satan continued, "*If* or *since* You are the Son of God, He will protect You. He will not dare let You be killed. That way, You can know just how far God will go to support You and give you His approval." What a thought!

"Besides," Satan prodded, "this would be a sure way of convincing a large number of people of Your power and God's approval. Certainly no one could argue with a miracle of this magnitude. Otherwise, how else will you be able to persuade the people that You are really the Son of God and the promised Messiah? *Who* is going to believe You if You go around quietly telling people to follow You, that You are the Messiah, God's Son?"

Very gently the Holy Spirit reminded Jesus that God had a plan for His life. Even though it would not be as spectacular or as popular, it was God's plan and would work—maybe slower but surer. Once again a passage of Scripture came to mind: "Do not put the Lord your God to the test."[4] Jesus had passed the test of "what people see and want"—the lust of the eyes.

With lightning speed Jesus was once more transported to a very high mountain. He beheld the grandeur of the panorama before Him. It was as if He could see all the kingdoms of the world in a glance. It was awesome! It was overwhelming! How big and powerful! How beautiful! "You can be the owner and ruler of all this if You want it. You can have a kingdom larger and more powerful than Solomon. You can have the adulation and control of almost all the people on the face of the earth. It won't be just a handful of people here in Palestine, but everyone on the face of the earth! I know how to do it, and all you have to do is fall down and worship me," said Satan.

Jesus looked around at everything again. How? This surely would please God—for Him to be able to bring all of these people before God and present them to Him as a gift. Instead of taking a lifetime of work on a small one-on-one basis, He could do it all with just one effort. What would He need to do? How would He go about it? "Why, I own them all, I'll give them to You," chuckled Satan. "All You have to do is just 'play ball' with me. You know what I mean—use my methods and learn from me. I can show You all the shortcuts. If You try to win the world with just goodness and love and wait for the Father to show You every little detail, it will take forever. And then some of those peoples and nations can't be won with love and a 'goody-goody' life. It will take strength and force to knock sense into some of them.

"Just think! You can have fame, popularity, and power. It is much easier this way than through grueling poverty, showing crowds, and discomfort. Of course, You will have to give me the credit for what I do, and let everyone know that You couldn't have done it without *my* help. A little compromise never hurt anyone. You wouldn't have to be a 'hard-liner,' and You could certainly live a lot easier. You could have more comfort and relax and enjoy a few good things in life while You are on the way through. After all, God made the good things to be enjoyed."

There was the temptation to cut corners. And Satan sounded so confident and sure of his methods and plans. He certainly made it sound inviting and all-inclusive. God promised Jesus the Son nothing like this. He Promised Jesus that He would have a hard struggle, that people would hesitate to follow Him, and that He couldn't hope to win the entire world. He would only have the prospects of winning and having the loyalty of a handful of mankind—not anything like the Messiah-King that the Jews had been taught to expect. But the prince Satan asked was too high. How could He possibly be the Messiah and God's beloved Son and swear allegiance to Satan? He couldn't do that to His Heavenly Father.

Jesus decided that He would be satisfied with what God gave Him and with the plan that God had laid out for His life. He would not think in terms of worldwide conquest for Himself now, although the complete plan of God included the whole world. He could not under any circumstances bring Himself to bow down and pay homage to Satan: God's self-acclaimed enemy. The Father loved Jesus. There was no way He could follow Satan's instructions and be faithful and loyal to God. Jesus was committed to a goal that was greater and higher—more difficult: that of true worship and devotion to God. God's way was harder, but the long-range results were guaranteed.

Begone, Satan! For it is written, "You shall worship the Lord your
God, and serve Him only."[5]

Jesus had passed the third ordeal—the pride of life, everything in this
world that people are so proud of.

Now the angels, which He would not permit to protect Him from
injury, came and ministered to Him.

Is this how things happened to Jesus? It happens like that in many
of our lives. Full of energy, plans, and ideals we embark upon life, only
to have Satan cast doubt on our salvation, motives, and direction—
confronting us with a "sure thing," a "shortcut," a "better deal," or
a "more logical path."

Whereas Jesus had His encounter with Satan, chose the better way,
and followed through to the end, we stumble along and when the
going gets rough, we reconsider the alternatives offered by Satan and
his cohorts. When we don't progress and reach the goals we have
established for ourselves, we once again face the temptations of this
world and seek a respite from turmoil and trouble in our lives by
dallying with the idea of accepting a limited amount of "ease" from
Satan.

Notes

1. Luke 3:22
2. Matthew 4:3-4
3. Matthew 4:6

4. Matthew 4:7, NIV
5. Matthew 4:10

3

A Stranger in His Own Home

After this He went down to Capernaum, He and His mother, and His brothers, and His disciples; and there they stayed a few days (John 2:12).

Family problems probably take first place when we mention problems. There are problems between husband and wife, parents and children, brothers and sisters and relatives. Problems! A lack of love, misunderstandings, jealousies, resentments, abandonment, or smothering! Because our lives are so closely entwined with those of our families, the problems related to family life sometimes assume a disproportionate importance in our lives.

If we have a family, we have problems. If we don't have a family, we have problems.

Would you believe that Jesus had some serious family problems? Jesus seemed to be thrust into His ministry faster than He wanted to be. He had been baptized and had been in the wilderness for forty days and nights. He had been in combat with the devil. He had chosen His disciples, taught in the synagogues, and preached to the crowds. He seemed to be moving along at a moderate pace until He went to the wedding in Cana with His disciples and His mother.

When the wine gave out at the wedding, His mother, conscious of her son's abilities and proud of His talents, appealed to Jesus.

"They have no wine."

"Why do you involve Me?" Jesus replied, "My hour has not yet come."[1] What was He saying? Was He not yet planning to begin this particular phase of His ministry? Had He wanted gradually to lead up to this work of the miracles? Did He feel He needed more prelimi-

23

nary activities before entering full-time into His ministry? But it was too late! His mother had already put Him on the spot.

"Do whatever he tells you,"[2] she had said to the servants. So there they stood awaiting His orders.

Jesus turned the water into the best wine at the festivities. This was a demonstration of a developed life habit. Whatever He was called on to do for others, Himself or the Father, He would make it the best. No "halfway" or "just-to-get-by" attitude. If it was worth doing, it was worth doing right. Why had the best wine been served last? Where had they found such good wine? Even the steward who was in charge was puzzled. But the servants knew, and they couldn't keep a secret. Jesus was responsible. He was in the limelight. Whether He was ready, whether He wanted to do it was of no consequence. Jesus *obeyed* His mother. His career was thrown into sensationalism.

After the wedding, Jesus and His mother and brothers and disciples went to Capernaum, Jesus' choice for a home base, to be together for a few days. We have no record of what they did, what was said, or the actual purpose of the retreat.

Did Jesus tell His family that He definitely was not going to return home to resume His old responsibilities and obligations—that His life had a new direction? Did He share with them His hopes, His plans, and His relationship with the Father? Did Jesus explain His mission and ask for their understanding, support, and cooperation?

We don't know the answers, but we do have some sad attitudes that evidently came about as a result. Whatever Jesus had hoped for apparently did not materialize.

Here are some of the examples about His family and their relationship afterwards:

> His mother came to Him and His brothers also, and they were unable to get to Him because of the crowd. And it was reported to Him, "Your mother and Your brothers are standing outside, *wishing to see You.*"

But He answered and said to them, "My mother and My brothers are these who hear the word of God and do it."³

Human family ties would not take precedence over His relationship with God the Father. It was not that Jesus loved His mother and brothers less, but that He loved God more. He realized that they didn't understand.

After this experience, Jesus traveled in Galilee. He did not want to travel in Judea because the Jewish authorities there were wanting to kill Him. The time for the Festival of Shelters was near, so Jesus' brothers advised Him:

Depart from here, and go into Judea, that Your disciples also may behold Your works which You are doing. For no one does anything in secret, when he himself seeks to be known publicly. If You do these things, show Yourself to the world.⁴

How this sarcasm and bitterness must have hurt Jesus. But He didn't defend Himself or lash back at their resentment. He quietly replied, "You go on to the festival. . . . the right time has not come for me."⁵ "For even his brothers did not believe in him"⁶

Then we have one of the most pathetic stories in the life of Jesus.

Then Jesus went home. Again such a large crowd gathered that Jesus and his disciples had no time to eat. When his family heard about it, they set out to take charge of him, because people were saying, "He's gone mad!"⁷

Later on in this same passage, Jesus had a discussion about Beelzebul and the expulsion of demons. He used an illustration that must have come from a heart heavy from recent experiences: "If a family divides itself into groups which fight each other, that family will fall apart."⁸

Sibling jealousy? Implications of mental breakdown? Sarcasm and resentment by family members? Embarassment at His way of life? His family didn't believe His claim to Messiahship and the anointing of God. How good it would have been to have a loving, accepting, and supportive family relationship. But His family, who knew Him intimately as son and brother, would not accept His claims to Messiahship. He was forced to look to His followers and His believers for the familial relationship. His parent was God the Father to whom He dedicated fellowship and filial devotion.

Notes

1. John 2:4
2. John 2:5, RSV
3. Luke 8:19-21 (author's italics)
4. John 7:3-5
5. John 7:8, GNB
6. John 7:5, RSV
7. Mark 3:20-21 GNB
8. Mark 3:25, GNB

4

No Silver Spoon

He was . . . rejected by men (Isa. 53:3*a*, NIV).
Is this not Joseph's son? (Luke 4:22).

Just because Jesus was God's Son, we must not fall into the error of believing that He led a privileged life—born with a silver spoon in His mouth. This was not the case. He developed a keen insight into human behavior and was able to use this knowledge to His advantage.

There is no doubt that Jesus knew where He was going and what the Lord, His Father, expected of Him. But often He may have been brought up short by the reactions of those around Him. If He knew what God wanted Him to do, how could those around Him be so blind? Why did they have so many doubts about what was right and wrong? Why were they more concerned about tradition or the opinion of others?

Many of Jesus's reactions need no comment. They speak for themselves as we quote from the Scriptures:

After looking around at them *with anger, grieved* at their hardness of heart.[1]
He *wondered* at their unbelief.[2]
He did not do many miracles there because of *their unbelief.*[3]

Even foreigners rejected Jesus. He and His disciples were on the way to Jerusalem, and they needed to pass through a Samaritan village. Jesus sent messengers ahead of Him to make preparations for them to stay: "But the people would not receive him"[4]

Did it matter that He was rejected, that even "seeing" they did not

27

believe? I believe so. He apparently expected them to believe and accept, otherwise why the words *grieved* and *wondered?* Many times in His trusting spirit He must have been flabbergasted by people's reactions to His message and Himself.

Jesus had just cleansed a demoniac and left him clothed and in his right mind. In the process of the cleansing, a herd of swine had rushed into the sea and drowned. Now one would assume that the townspeople would be overjoyed at the restoration of a human being to sanity and society. But not so! The people came out of the city to meet Jesus. "And everyone begged Jesus to go away and leave them alone."[5] Jesus wasn't expecting a reward or recognition. He, Himself, had said, 'I am not looking for human praise."[6]

Nevertheless, He was thrown out of town.

Oh, yes! Jesus knew what it meant to be rejected and to be rudely received. Even though He knew He was the Son of God, the wordly wise found in Him a "maybe" prophet or an amusing attraction.

Jesus had been invited to the home of a Pharisee for dinner. After He was seated at the table, a woman of the world, "a sinner," came in and began to weep. Her tears fell copiously over Jesus' feet. She noticed that His feet were wet with her tears and quickly but gently took her long tresses and wiped away the tears. Afterwards she anointed His feet with ointment from an alabaster flask she had brought.

Jesus looked at Simon who perhaps was smirking and perceived his thoughts: "If this man were a prophet He would know who and what sort of person this woman is who is touching Him, that she is a sinner."[7]

"Simon," Jesus said, "I have something to say to you." With mock courtesy Simon responded: "Say it, Teacher."

Jesus, in His gracious but firm manner, told a story: "A man loaned money to two people—$5,000 to one and $500 to the other. But neither of them could pay him back, so he kindly forgave them both, letting them keep the money!" Then Jesus asked a pointed question, "Which of them therefore will love him more?"

Simon was a bit disconcerted. "I suppose," he answered, "the one whom he forgave more."

"How right you are," Jesus said. "Do you remember that when I entered your house, *you didn't offer Me the courtesy of water for My feet?* But this woman has washed My feet and dried them. Simon, do you remember when I entered your home, *you did not give Me the customary kiss of greeting,* but this woman has kissed and anointed My feet. You see, Simon, she is a sinful woman, but her sins have been forgiven. She was merely expressing her gratitude for forgiveness."

Now wouldn't you think the religious leaders would applaud and compliment the Teacher on His wisdom and act of gracious spirit? But it didn't happen that way at all. They whispered behind their hands to each other: "Who does He think He is?" and, "He believes He can forgive sins."

Jesus turned to the woman, "Your faith has saved you; go in peace."[8]

Rejection was not new to Jesus. In His earlier ministry He made a trip to His hometown: Nazareth. It was His habit to go to the synagogue on the sabbath. How good it must have been to visit His home synagogue, the place of so many happy childhood memories. If anyone would be pleased to see Him, proud of His accomplishments, surely it would be His old friends and relations!

As He expected, He was invited to the front to read from the sacred scrolls. It was actually at God's leading that the scroll of Isaiah was given to Him. He could share with them the glorious news that he was the Messiah. Surely they would rejoice with Him and support Him as He spread the good news. He read:

> The Spirit of the Lord is upon Me,
> Because He anointed Me to preach the gospel to the poor.
> He has sent Me to proclaim release to the captives,

And recovery of sight to the blind,
To set free those who are down trodden,
To proclaim the favorable year of the Lord.[9]

Jesus rolled up the scroll and handed it back to the attendant. His eyes were brilliant and His face glowed. Everyone in the synagogue gazed at Him intently. "Friends," Jesus said, "today you have seen these Scriptures fulfilled."[10]

They heard, but they didn't understand. "What lovely words," some exclaimed. "Didn't Joseph's son do well?" asked others. "He's not so special," snorted a few. "We know His mother and brothers and sisters. Where did He get all that knowledge and training?"

Then he said, "Probably you will quote me that proverb, 'Physician, heal yourself'—meaning, 'Why don't you do miracles here in your home town like those you did in Capernaum?' But I solemnly declare to you that no prophet is accepted in his own home town! For example, remember how Elijah the prophet used a miracle to help the widow of Zarephath—a foreigner from the land of Sidon. There were many Jewish widows needing help in those days of famine, for there had been no rain for three-and-one-half years, and hunger stalked the land; yet Elijah was not sent to one of them. Or think of the prophet Elisha, who healed Naaman, a Syrian, rather than the many Jewish lepers needing help."[11]

What an affront for Jesus to tell them these stories! What was He trying to prove? Was He telling them they were not good enough to see and be a part of His miracles? Was He rejecting His hometown people and relations? Apparently, they thought so.

Suddenly, they were furious! Imagine this local boy coming back here thinking that He had a special contact with God, thinking *He* could sit in judgment over them! Why, He even hinted that He was the Messiah. That was blasphemy! There was only one way to take care of someone like Him. They would teach Him a lesson that would not easily be forgotten.

They rushed Him out of the city. But there were some who went further and intended to throw Him over the side of the mountain to kill Him.

Jesus was stunned! His lifelong friends and acquantances did not merely reject Him and His message: they wanted to kill Him! In the confusion and milling around, Jesus passed through the midst of them and went away.

Jesus knew rejection and humiliation not only from family, friends, and enemies, but He also felt rejection of town after town. Once despair overcame Him as He looked down on the city of Jerusalem, the Holy City of David:

> O Jerusalem, Jerusalem, who kills the prophets and stones those who are sent to her! How often I wanted to gather your children together, the way a hen gathers her chicks under her wings, and you were unwilling.[12]

What a great temptations it could have been to "wring His hands" and bemoan the fact that "no one loves Me or appreciates Me." But Jesus' sense of mission kept His thoughts off His own personal problems and on God's commission.

Notes

1. Mark 3:5 (author's italics)
2. Mark 6:6 (author's italics)
3. Matthew 13:58 (author's italics)
4. Luke 9:52-53, RSV
5. Luke 8:37, TLB
6. John 5:41, GNB
7. Luke 7:39
8. Luke 7:41-50, TLB (Author's paraphrase)
9. Luke 4:18-19
10. Luke 4:21 (Author's paraphrase)
11. Luke 4:23-27, TLB
12. Matthew 23:37

5

Lonely Again

A man of sorrows, and acquainted with grief (Isa. 53:3*b*).
He withdrew . . . to a lonely place by Himself (Matt. 14:13).

Jesus knew about sorrow, trouble, and heartbreak. He knew from
firsthand experiences. He cautioned His disciples so they would not
fret, worry, or think it strange when they had similar experiences.

Jesus had discovered for Himself the way to peace. Having found
the answer, He wanted to share it with those He loved best.

These things I have spoken to you, that in Me you may have peace. In
the world you have tribulation, but take courage; I have overcome the
world.[1]

Jesus wept, grieved, sought quiet and solitude. He was concerned
for His family, His friends, even those who rejected Him. He wanted
so very much to help each one and lead everyone to the right way.
There was an answer to their problems if they would just let Him
direct them.

Jesus treasured His few moments of quiet time and privacy. Many
times while His companions were sleeping or resting, He stole away
to a solitary place for prayer and communion with His Father:

After bidding them farewell, He departed to the mountain to pray.[2]

When He had entered a house, He wanted no one to know of it; yet
He could not escape notice.[3]

In the early morning, *while it was still dark,* He arose and went out and
departed to a lonely place, and was praying there.[4]

They went on from there and passed through Galilee. And *he would not have any one know it;* for he was teaching his disciples."[5]

There is a time when most people like to be alone—on receiving the news of the death of a loved one:

Although he was grieved, the king . . . sent and had John beheaded in the prison. . . . And his disciples came and took away the body and buried it; and they went and reported to Jesus. Now when Jesus heard it, *He withdrew from there* in a boat, to a *lonely place by Himself.*[6]

The love and compassion Jesus felt for people was given first place and overrode His own personal grief and need.

Have you ever noticed two or more people in a lively conversation close by, and as they talk, they keep looking over in your direction to see if you are listening or hearing the discussion? Jesus knew the feeling of being left out—deliberately, unmistakenly not included:

They came to Capernaum; and when He was in the house, He began to question them, "What were you discussing on the way?" But they kept silent, for on the way they had discussed with one another which of them was the greatest.[7]

A discussion on a subject not approved by Jesus could certainly not be told, but even though they didn't tell Jesus, He knew. For didn't He tell them the right attitude to assume without rebuking them about their own bickering?

And sitting down, He called the twelve and said to them, "If anyone wants to be first, he shall be last of all, and servant of all."[8]

Jesus got the "silent treatment." What a temptation it could have been to lash out and "preach" right attitudes. Or maybe it would have been more dramatic to give them the "cold shoulder" and act "peeved."

Jesus' friends were embarrassed by His words and actions. He was disdained by His own family, who did not recognize in Him anything other than a member of the family with "peculiarities."

Was Jesus insensitive to the actions and feelings of His own family and friends? He must have sensed their shame and embarrassment because of Him. How deeply were His own personal feelings affected? He was human: it must have hurt intensely.

Jesus needed the support of His own family, but didn't receive it. Did it make Him bitter? Did He reject His family to "get even?" Did He try to prove that He didn't need them? I don't believe so. One of the last concerns He had just before He died was the care of His mother.

Another time He was with His brothers when they taunted Him about being seen and admired by the crowds. If He had rejected His brothers, would they have joined the disciples voluntarily and readily after His death and resurrection?

Time was running out for Jesus. Things were happening to quickly. Jesus had just narrowly avoided being stoned and later imprisoned. He went away across the Jordan River to the place where John had first baptized. He was teaching His disciples. He had already told them about His coming death, burial, and resurrection. He knew He would suffer. Prisoners were always beaten, ridiculed, reviled, and insulted. And the cross! Jesus had no illusions about the cross. He knew it was a ghastly, excruciating death. He shuddered with shame, knowing that the criminals were stripped of their clothing and exposed to the crowd. Pressure was building. There was still so much to teach His followers, so many new truths to tell them, as well as a review of the basics. The crowd was always present. He couldn't even walk in the cities anymore: he had to keep to the fields and open places because of the multitude.

Then the word came from Bethany, "Come quickly! Lazarus, Your beloved friend is very sick." Ah, Lazarus! Brother of Mary and Martha! But the Father had already revealed to Jesus what He must do. He must again raise someone from the dead in order to reaffirm His position as the Resurrection and the Life—*the only Way* to God the Father.

How Martha must be fretting—standing at the door watching, asking every few minutes if there was a word from the Master. And Mary! She would be off alone trying to justify to herself the reasons why Jesus was delaying. *Jesus would not let us down—not at a time like this—not Jesus, our family's closest friend!*

Jesus looked at His disciples and sighed. Even they didn't understand. "If Lazarus is only sleeping why worry?" After all, they were frankly afraid. Only a short time before the Jews had just tried to stone Jesus in Jerusalem. So Jesus told them, "Lazarus is dead. . . . but let us go to him." Thomas, you know, the Doubter, said to his fellow disciples, "Let us also go, that we may die with Him." (How sad that not many people remember this facet of Thomas's personality—the bravery—but choose only to remember his doubting attitude after Jesus' resurrection.)

Jesus dreaded arriving in Bethany. He knew Martha would attack head-on when He arrived. But Martha was level-headed, and after "spouting off," she would quickly see the deeper meaning and understand the reasons behind His delay. And she did. When word came, "Jesus is here," Martha rushed out to meet Him and immediately rebuked Him. But, as Jesus already knew, she quickly turned to a beautiful conversation with a firm statement of faith and recognition.

But where was Mary? Jesus was disappointed. "When Martha got word that Jesus was coming, she went to meet him. *But Mary stayed at home.*" [9]

Martha went to Mary—Mary, the one who so loved and believed in Jesus that she hung on His every word; Mary, the one who adored Him, even being willing to endure a tongue-lashing by Martha just to be near Him; Mary, the gentle one, the understanding one. But when Mary came, Jesus saw that she didn't understand either. She lashed out at Him like Martha, saying the same words. But coming from

Mary, they probably wounded him more. He spoke to her in reassuring tones with words of comfort and hope.

But He had been hurt. The one that should have understood and stood by and accepted Him and His decisions had resented His delay —had blamed Him for her brother's death. Mary was beligerent— Mary, the kind and mild one. "Jesus wept."[10] Perhaps it was a combination of many things: exhaustion, hurt, rejection, pressure, time, urgency, disappointment. Together they weighed down upon Him. He looked at Mary. He looked around at all those who had come with her.

> When Jesus saw her weeping, and the Jews who had come along with her also weeping, he was deeply moved in spirit and troubled. . . . Jesus, once more deeply moved, came to the tomb.[11]

Those who were in the crowd saw only the outward appearance of Jesus talking with Lazarus's sisters, and they said, "See how he loved him!" But was Jesus weeping only because of Lazarus's death? He *knew* that Lazarus would be raised to life. This He knew *before* Lazarus died. But there were critics also: Couldn't the one who opened the eyes of the blind also have kept Lazarus from dying?

Jesus, being deeply moved again, went to the tomb and asked that the stone be removed. Martha again rebuked Him, reminding Him of how long her brother had been dead. This time Jesus spoke a little more firmly: "Martha, did I not tell you that if you believe you would see the glory of God?" Then Jesus looked heavenward to the only One who really cared or understood:

> Father, I thank Thee that Thou heardest Me. And I knew that Thou hearest Me always; but because of the people standing around I said it, that they may believe that Thou didst send Me.[12]

Then Jesus cried out with a loud voice, "Lazarus, come forth." After Lazarus had emerged into the daylight, Jesus instructed, "Unbind him, and let him go."

Immediately, some of the neighbors and friends who had seen everything ran with a report to the Pharisees. And Jesus slipped away to the town of Ephraim with His disciples.

I imagine that Mary was ashamed. What made her attack Jesus as she had? She cried as she remembered the hurt look in His eyes, the shock of her unexpected attitude and words. She knew He was deeply disappointed. He had thought she understood, but in her grief and hurt she had vented her feelings on Jesus—her beloved Jesus!

Now Mary wanted to show Jesus how sorry she was. She must let Him know that she loved Him and didn't mean to hurt Him. And for herself, she had to know that she was forgiven—that He understood and had not rejected her. But how? He had gone, leaving soon after Lazarus emerged from the tomb.

Word came that Jesus would be attending a banquet at the home of Simon, the leper in Bethany.[13] Lazarus was also going to be present, and Martha was going to help serve. What could Mary do? *I must see Him. I must let Him know how sorry I am. I know!* she thought. She rushed out and bought a beautiful alabaster jar filled with expensive, perfumed ointment. She had hurt Him in private, but she would ask for His forgiveness in public! She was excited. She would show everyone how much she loved Jesus.

The banquet had started, and everyone was busy talking and eating. Mary looked into the room. Ah, yes! There was Jesus at the place of honor. She slipped into the room. She would break the expensive bottle to pour out the perfume so everyone could see that this was an homage to Jesus. The bottle of ointment was for Him and Him alone —never again would the beautiful bottle be used for anyone or anything else.

Mary saw by the look in His eyes that He understood she was asking for forgiveness. In her happiness, she almost didn't hear when those close to Jesus began to berate her and criticize her. She had thought that everyone would be happy with the gift she was offering.

After all, wasn't the banquet in honor of Jesus? "So they made Him a supper there."[14] Wasn't *He* the one to receive the applause and attention for the evening?

And then she heard Jesus saying: "Leave her alone! Why are you bothering her? She had done a fine and beautiful thing for me. . . . She did what she could."[15]

Some said to themselves indignantly, "What was the use of wasting the perfume? It could have been sold for more than three hundred silver coins and the money given to the poor!"[16]

Mary's heart sang! Jesus had accepted her offering: her apology. She was forgiven! Jesus said: "Truly I say to you, wherever the gospel is preached in the whole world, that also which this woman has done shall be spoken of in memory of her."[17]

Jesus chose to ignore the personal, degrading remarks of those at the banquet. He was so interested in forgiving and protecting another that He could overlook the insults to Himself.

How often we as believers blame Jesus because He doesn't do what we want Him to do. How often we pout and decide to quit praying, reading the Bible, or going to church because the Lord doesn't meet our timetable or resolve a problem to our liking. Those of us who pride ourselves on "sitting at the feet of Jesus"—how many times have we also "lashed out" at Him, and then repentant, worked overtime trying to prove and reaffirm our love for Him?

Notes

1. John 16:33
2. Mark 6:46
3. Mark 7:24-25 (author's italics)
4. Mark 1:35, (author's italics)
5. Mark 9:30, RSV (author's italics)
6. Matthew 14:9-14 (author's italics)
7. Mark 9:33-34
8. Mark 9:35
9. John 11:20, TLB (author's italics)
10. John 11:35

11. John 11:33, 38, NIV
12. John 11:41-42, 44
13. Mark 14:3-9
14. John 12:2

15. Mark 14:6, GNB
16. Mark 14:4, GNB
17. Mark 14:9

6

Rejected

Scorned by men and despised by the people (Ps. 22:6, NIV).
I do not know this man (Mark 14:71, RSV).

How it hurts to have our words doubted, our methods questioned, and our motives mistrusted. Criticism and mockery are certain to send us into depression and self-ridiculed examination or resentment. No one likes to be ridiculed. No one enjoys having his/her authority challenged. Jesus faced all of these unsettling problems. He had all the elements together for a real "hate case" against certain people and sects, but He did not fall victim to the temptation.

Jesus had been on the Mount of Transfiguration. There the Father had reaffirmed His love and Jesus' true identity. There the Father had said, "This is My beloved Son, Listen to Him!"[1] After having His spirit nurtured by the Heavenly Father, Jesus went down into the valley to the other disciples. He joined a waiting crowd and immediately a man rushed up to Him saying, "Teacher, I brought my son for you to heal . . . I begged your disciples to cast out the demon but they couldn't do it . . . do something if you can."[2]

Jesus had just had a mountaintop experience in the truest sense of the words, and the first problem He met when He returned was the barb of an irritated "doubting Thomas" who threw cold water on Him and tried to quench the Spirit. Jesus did not miss the insinuation about His capability: "If You can?" A very human reaction would have been for Jesus to say, "Sorry, but I only help those who have unfaltering faith. Evidently you don't qualify."

But Jesus saw a greater challenge than defending a wounded ego.

He saw a suffering child. He cast out the demon that had bound the lad, with the instruction that it was never to enter him again. After crying out and convulsing the child terribly, the demon came out, and the boy was like a corpse. Most of them gasped out, "He is dead." I can picture Jesus' loving concern as He reached down, took the lad by the hand, and "helped him to his feet and he stood up and was all right!"[3]

It is demoralizing for us to be self-confident of our positions and have someone throw out to the crowd a simple, little insinuating word—*if*.

Have you been laughed at or ridiculed, especially when you were serious? Jesus had gone to the house of one of the rulers of the synagogue to heal the gravely ill only child of that family. As he was going, a huge crowd followed Him. In this crowd the woman with "an issue of blood believed, touched Jesus, and was healed." When Jesus sensed that special powers had gone out of Him for the healing, He asked who had touched Him. The disciples quickly patronized Him, saying in so many words, "You must be joking! You see the crowd pressing around You, yet You say: 'Who touched Me?' "

This time Jesus chose to ignore the biting sarcasm of His companions. He pressed ahead to the ruler's home. Someone from the house came rushing up to tell them that it was too late. The little girl was dead. But Jesus addressed Himself to the ruler of the synagogue, "Do not fear, only believe." When He entered the house there was a bedlam of moaning, wailing people. He looked around and inquired, "Why do you make a tumult and weep? The child is not dead, but sleeping."

They *laughed* at Him! Jesus had never been so serious. He was still feeling the sting of His disciples' jibes. Now the people were openly ridiculing—laughing at Him. Jesus put them all outside except the child's parents and went to where the little girl lay. "Taking the child by the hand, He said to her, . . . 'Little girl, I say to you, arise!' "[4]

Immediately, the girl arose and walked. Then tender-hearted, caring Jesus reminded the parents that she needed something to eat.

Criticism and censure from others are especially difficult pills to swallow. Jesus was criticized by His followers, His family, acquaintances, and strangers. For many people, it is easier to find fault with another person than to examine his motives and actions and accept him as he is. Such was the case of the Pharisees, Sadducees, and scribes in Jesus' day. What an encouragement it could have been to have the approval of the religious leaders and authorities of that day, but their attitude was one of complete rejection. They wanted to destroy Jesus.

> The man went away, and told the Jews that it was Jesus who had made him well. And for this reason *the Jews were persecuting Jesus,* because He was doing these things on the Sabbath. . . . For this cause therefore *the Jews were seeking all the more to kill Him.*[5]

Slander has always been a tool of the devil in trying to hurt God's servants. Jesus did not escape this type of offense. As a matter of fact, He knew about the charges and made reference to them in one of His public discourses. He suffered comparisons with other religious leaders and what was worse, with a relative. As He was speaking He used this illustration:

> For John came neither eating nor drinking, and they say, "He has a demon!" The Son of Man came eating and drinking, and they say, *"Behold, a gluttonous man and a drunkard, a friend of tax-gathers and sinners!"*[6]

> The Jews answered and said to Him, "Do we not say rightly that *You are a Samaritan and have a demon?"*[7]

Throughout these experiences we never hear Jesus saying, "I can't please everyone," or "No one understands Me." We do not hear Him justifying His actions or words to His critics. He did not dignify their criticism by responding to it. Nevertheless, He was interested in the disciples' interpretation of what they were seeing and hearing.

After casting out demons, healing the sick, restoring the lepers, feeding five thousand people with five loaves of bread and two fishes, raising the dead, and giving sight to the blind, Jesus asked this question: "Who are the people saying I am?"

It was only natural that Jesus wanted to find out from His closest friends exactly what the people were thinking and saying. What did His disciples think about all that they had seen and heard? How much had really penetrated their thinking as to Jesus' true identity. After hearing their response, He then wanted to know the opinion of His companions: "Who do *you* think I am?"[8] It was good to hear from their own lips, "You are the Messiah, the Son of the living God" (GNB).

This does not necessarily mean that Jesus needed the approval of the crowd, His disciples, and family, but it was a gauge for evaluating the progress of His program of work. Note that He only asked people who were very intimate with Him and His work. The first time it was His disciples. Another time it was a dear and trusted friend, Martha:

> I am the resurrection and the life; he who believes in Me shall live even
> if he dies, and everyone who lives and believes in Me shall never die.
> Do you believe this?[9]

The question was the same one put to the disciples, "Who do you say that I am?" How gratifying Martha's answer must have been to one who was becoming more and more accustomed to rejection: "I have believed that You are the Christ, the Son of God, even He who comes into the world" (John 11:27).

Guess who spoke the words: "I do not know this fellow you are talking about!"[10] It was none other than Peter—one of Jesus' first disciples, a leader among the other disciples, one of the inner circle. Aren't we, today's modern Christians, just as prone to pretend that we don't know Jesus when we are under pressure from the world and questioned about our faith?

In spite of the disciples' great protestations of faith and acceptance, there were occasions when they belittled and disparaged Jesus. The Pharisees and scribes once came to Jesus and asked Him if He were aware that the disciples were breaking tradition by not washing properly before eating. Jesus immediately and openly defended His disciples and turned the accusations against the accusers. Afterwards the disciples came to him and said, "Do you know that the Pharisees were offended when they heard this statement?"[11]

No "thank You for taking up for us" or other word of appreciation, just a reproof for speaking too harshly to His confessed enemies.

Jesus knew what it was to be personally attacked by outsiders over and over again. "The Pharisees come out and *began to argue* with Him, . . . *to test Him*. . . . sighing deeply in His spirit"[12]

Many passages show the same theme: Jesus was persecuted, threatened, tested, and plotted against repeatedly. This was not a one-time happening in His life. This was a *way of life!* How many people can take attack after attack without reacting negatively or becoming depressed and defeated? Yet Jesus succeeded in doing precisely that.

Possibly one of the unkindest attacks to His person came from His disciples. Maybe it seemed just a little thing to them. It may be they didn't intend it like it sounded. It could be they were caught up in the moment with a desire to show a social awareness. Nevertheless, the harsh words issued from the lips of His companions.

Jesus was at the house of Simon the Leper. While He was at the table eating, a woman came in with a jar of expensive ointment. She broke the jar and poured the ointment over His head. What was the reaction of those around Him? Mark tells us that some of the disciples "said to themselves indignantly, 'Why was the ointment thus wasted?' "[13] Notice first that they "said to themselves" (indicating that Jesus, sensitive to the thoughts and attitudes of others, had perceived what they were thinking or whispering among themselves and felt their indignation). They thought that something good and expensive was *wasted* on Jesus. But the important fact to remember is: although Jesus was belittled in their thoughts, He was more concerned about the hurt and rebuke that the woman felt, and He defended her publicly.

Problems, problems, problems! Jesus was surrounded by problems, pursued by problems, but not overcome by problems. Many times little irritations can become major problems if they are not handled properly. For example, it is an aggravation to ask a direct question and get an indirect response of whining self-pity:

> When Jesus saw him lying there, and knew that he had already been a long time in that condition, He said to him, "Do you wish to get well?" The sick man answered Him, "Sir I have no man to put me into the pool when the water is stirred up' "[14]

Jesus didn't ask: "Why are you waiting here?" He didn't question the man about his problems or his family. He asked a simple, direct question: "Do you want to get well?" The man could have simply replied: "Yes, Master." But he didn't. He felt sorry for himself, so he whimpered, "Poor little me! No one cares about me! I have no one to help me." So many times we become irritated with someone (especially in the family) who will not give us a direct answer to a simple, direct question. But Jesus didn't let these "little" things detour Him from the more important issue at hand—the person's need. He refused to be bogged down by petty irritations. Annoyances which manage to upset too many of us were common, everyday occurences to Jesus. He had His own timetable, His own goals, and His own purpose which helped Him keep the right perspective in the face of aggravations.

Often were the times that Jesus' word, His requests, and His desires were ignored for whatever reason, however good it may have seemed at the time. Jesus often did things He asked to be kept secret—that the recipient of a special blessing or miracle keep the act in confidence, not revealing the source:

But the Pharisees went out, and counseled together against Him, as to how they might destroy Him. But Jesus, aware of this, withdrew from there. And many followed Him, and He healed them all, and *warned them not to make Him known.*[15]

A leper came to Jesus asking for healing, and Jesus

stretched out His hand and touched him, and said to him, "I am willing; be cleansed." . . . And He sternly warned him and immediately sent him away, and He said to him, *"See that you say nothing to anyone;"* . . . *But he went out and began to proclaim it freely and to spread the news about, to such an extent that Jesus could no longer publicly enter a city, but stayed out in unpopulated areas.*[16]

Another time two blind men were following Jesus, calling aloud for mercy and healing. Jesus entered a house, and the blind men came in to Him. Jesus asked if they had faith to believe He could heal them. They answered yes.

Then He touched their eyes, saying, "Be it done to you according to your faith." And their eyes were opened. And Jesus sternly warned them, saying, *"See here, let no one know about this!" But they went out, and spread the news about Him in all that land.*[17]

Jesus was already under threat of death from the Jews. He still had many things he wanted to do and teach, so He asked for cooperation from those who had received His healing. But they either forgot or were too elated over their good fortune to keep quiet. Surely they didn't understand the implications of disobedience of such an innocent-sounding request. Their disobedience hastened the day of Jesus' death, as well as hampered His daily work.

Jesus worked under the authority of God. But those of the religious hierarchy could not understand the actions of a man who would or could work without their blessing and consent. They kept testing Jesus, but finally their exasperation got the best of them. They demanded to know where Jesus got the authority for all He was doing.

> As He was walking in the temple, the chief priests, and scribes, and elders came to Him, and began saying to Him, "By what authority are You doing these things, or who gave You this authority to do these things?"[18]

Jesus dared to question the existing religious system of revenue. He was deeply grieved over the irreverence he found with reference to the things of God. From the *Harmony of the Gospels,* the compiler indicated that there were at least two cleansings of the Temple. The writer of John's Gospel made the other incident even more dramatic and impressive:

> The Passover of the Jews was at hand, and Jesus went up to Jerusalem. And He found in the temple those who were selling oxen and sheep and doves, and the moneychangers seated. And He made a scourge of cords, and drove them all out of the temple, with the sheep and the oxen; and He poured out the coins of the moneychangers, and overturned their tables; and to those who were selling the doves He said, "Take these things away; stop making My Father's house a house of merchandise."[19]

Why did Jesus take such violent action in the Temple? Under the authority of God, was Jesus starting a chain reaction that would culminate in His death? Or did the activities, so contrary to the teachings of God, so revolt Him that He felt compelled to take action? When did Jesus plan this action, or did He think of it at the moment He saw all that was going on and then take time to make the whip? The fact that Jesus did the cleansing in plain view of the people put the leaders on the defensive and initiated the final retaliation that would bring about His crucifixion. Jesus' first loyalty was to God and the sacred affairs of the kingdom. It required daring and courage to confront the religious hierarchy. Jesus knew it would bring about grave problems, but He also knew He was right.

Jesus not only met and dealt with irritations, inconveniences, and aggravations, but He was called on to face a deep soul searching and struggle over an insurmountable problem. Jesus knew what it was to agonize over a problem. He was in the garden of Gethsemane with His disciples. He had called to those closest to Him: Peter, James, and John:

> And he said to them, "My soul is very sorrowful, even to death;" . . . And going a little farther, he fell on the ground and prayed that, if it were possible, the hour might pass from him. And he said, "Abba Father, all things are possible to thee; remove this cup from me; yet not what I will, but what thou wilt."[20]

The fact that the author used the word *fell* instead of knelt shows the intensity of Jesus' emotions in regards to this monumental crisis. His words *sorrowful, even to death* indicate the depth of His personal suffering and anguish—the gravity of the problem: When Jesus needed His disciples more than ever, they went to sleep. He had just told them how concerned He was: "Sorrowful, even to death." But they didn't understand that He was pleading for their support, asking them to stand by Him. They were tired—perhaps with physical weariness; maybe it was mental and emotional fatigue. They couldn't keep their eyes open; they slept.

Twice Jesus came back. Instead of finding them wide awake, deep in prayer, and also imploring the Father for strength and special care for their Friend, He found them asleep. Jesus was disappointed, hurt, and resigned. If ever there was a reason to give up—throw up His hands and quit—this could have been the "straw that broke the camel's back." But Jesus had turned His face and His destiny toward God and the Cross, and He wouldn't turn back. He knew then that He walked a lonely way, and the only One who could help Him now was His Heavenly Father.

Notes

1. Mark 9:7
2. Mark 9:17-22, TLB
3. Mark 9:25-27, TLB
4. Mark 5:30,42
5. John 5:15-18 (author's italics); 8:37; 8:40; 8:59; 10:31; 10:39, RSV; 11:53
6. Matt. 11:18-19 (author's italics)
7. John 8:48 (author's italics)
8. Matthew 16:15, TLB
9. John 11:25-26
10. Mark 14:71
11. Matthew 15:12
12. Mark 8:11-12; 12:2; 12:13; 12:15*b*; Matthew 12:10; 19:3; Matthew 22:15,18 RSV; 26:3-4
13. Mark 14:3-9, RSV
14. John 5:6-7
15. Matthew 12:14-16 (author's italics)
16. Mark 1:40-45 (author's italics)
17. Matthew 9:27-31 (author's italics)
18. Mark 11:27-28
19. John 2:13-18
20. Mark 14:34-36, RSV

7

The Pressure Cooker

Our sorrows He carried (Isa. 53:4).
But be on your guard. (Mark 13:9).

In the Gospel of Mark we see the urgency and pressure under which Jesus lived and worked. In the first three chapters of this Book, we find the word *immediately* used nine times. Much of His life was not an organized series of events, but "as He went,"[1] and "as Jesus passed on from there,"[2] "While He was saying these things,"[3] "He was passing through,"[4] "While He was still speaking,"[5] "while He was praying alone."[6] Life came about as He was busy living it. For Him there was no neatly arranged schedule with a specific hour to begin or to end a day; no time for Him to "close up shop" and go home.

In today's world we all suffer from busy schedules and lack of time. How we fret over appointments, engagements, and schedules. Jesus also faced the problem of not enough hours in the day to do all that needed to be done. We read that He became tired and tried to escape the rat race from time to time.

And when He had entered a house, He wanted no one to know of it; yet He could not escape notice.[7]

When He had come back to Capernaum several days afterward, it was heard that He was at home. And many were gathered together, so that there was no longer room, even near the door.[8]

He came home, and the multitude gathered again, to such an extent that they could not even eat a meal.[9]

When day came, He departed and went to a lonely place; and the multitudes were searching for Him, and came to Him, and tried to keep Him from going away from them.[10]

If anyone was a number-one candidate for burnout from exhaustion because of work overload, it was Jesus. We do not find an attitude of resentment or rebellion in Jesus because His main thought was not for Himself and His rights, His opportunities, or His privileges. The love and compassion He felt for people and His sense of mission were given first place and overrode His own personal feelings, needs, and rights.

It is hard to live constantly in the public eye, especially when the public dogs one's steps from early morning until late at night, as was true in Jesus' case. The multitudes at times became unruly mobs, and Jesus even had concern for His own safety. The Scriptures tell us:

> So many thousands of the multitude had gathered together that they trod upon one another.[11]

> Jesus withdrew to the sea with His disciples: and a great multitude from Galilee followed; and also from Judea, and from Jerusalem, and from Idumea, and beyond the Jordan, and the vicinity of Tyre and Sidon, a great multitude heard of all that He was doing and came to Him. And He told His disciples that a boat should stand ready for Him because of the multitude, in order that they might not crowd Him[12]

The Revised Standard Version uses the phrase: "lest they should crush him."

It is terrifying to be caught up in a multitude and fear for your life. There are many instances even in today's world of people being crushed to death by a mob or trampled to death by rushing throngs.

Instead of separating Himself from the mobs, Jesus saw an opportunity for teaching the message of God:

> That same day Jesus went out of the house and sat beside the sea. And great crowds gathered about him, so that he got into a boat and sat there; and the whole crowd stood on the beach. And he told them many things in parables.[13]

Another time, realizing the shortness of His allotted time, *"He called the people to him* and said to them, "Hear and understand."[14]

"As They were coming down the mountain, . . . *they came to the crowd."*[15] It is interesting to note that although the crowds followed Jesus, they were jealous of His time given to others along the way:

> As they were going out from Jericho, a great multitude followed Him. And behold, two blind men sitting by the road, . . . cried out, saying "Lord, have mercy on us" . . . *And the multitude sternly told them to be quiet.*[16]

Jesus also had compassion for the individual who came to Him in desperation and faith.

> When He had entered a house, He wanted no one to know of it; yet He could not escape notice. But after hearing of Him, a woman whose little daughter had an unclean spirit, immediately came and fell at His feet.[17]

What right did a Gentile woman have to come barging into the house with a request? Didn't He already have so much to do that He couldn't even find time to eat? And speaking of eating, how dare she come at mealtime? Hadn't she noticed that Jesus was only working with the Jews? She was making a nuisance of herself. Have you ever had these thoughts as you read the story of the Syrophoenician woman? The disciples, filled with self-importance told Jesus, "Send her away, for she is shouting out after us."

I was sent only to the lost sheep of the house of Israel. There are never enough hours in the day to take care of everyone who needs help. A person has to draw the line somewhere. I can't be expected to do everything. Jesus *could* have had these thoughts. After all, haven't we many times lashed out at someone for expecting too much of us, for inconveniencing us at mealtime or when we were tired? And to add insult to injury, she was a foreigner!

But Jesus was always sensitive to another's need. Jesus spoke,

"Because of your faith and attitude, I have already healed your daughter. You can go home." (Author's paraphrase).

Jesus was concerned about the problems that He forsaw for His disciples and followers. He tried to warn them, to prepare them for the dark days and unknown roads that were ahead. He knew His own future was dark and bleak, but He pushed this knowledge to the background as He educated His companions in the ways of the kingdom of God. He was concerned about the feelings of His disciples and the pressures under which they lived. He realized that though they tried they just didn't quite comprehend the future and the deeper aspects of Jesus' teachings and ministry. Jesus was many times exasperated and aggravated with them, but so many times He was also considerate and gentle with those who walked with Him day after day in loyalty and zeal.

> He would say to them, "Come away by yourselves to a lonely place and rest a while." (For there were many people coming and going, and they did not even have time to eat.)[18]

> About the fourth watch of the night he came to them, walking on the sea. He meant to pass by them, but when they saw him walking on the sea they thought it was a ghost, and cried out; for they all saw him, and were terrified. But immediately he spoke to them and said, "Take heart, it is I; have no fear." And he got into the boat with them.[19]

Jesus also tried to protect His disciples from the same type criticism that He endured. He sensed that His disciples were criticized because it was one way of indirectly attacking Him.

Jesus was anxious that His disciples understand what He was saying, and why He was saying it. He did not speak to the people without a parable, "but *He was explaining everything privately to His own disciples.*"[20]

Jesus was distressed when they could not seem to remember or comprehend. "*Do you not yet perceive or understand? Are your hearts* hardened? Having eyes do you not see, and having ears *"do you not hear? And do you not remember?"* [21]

Jesus often acted as a loving parent to His disciples as He warned them, coached them, cautioned them, encouraged them, advised them, and alerted them. I have used several different passages to give an idea of the number of times and ways that Jesus taught them: Jesus began to say to them, *"See to it that no one misleads you."* [22]

"Beware of practicing your righteousness before men to be noticed by them; otherwise you have no reward with your Father who is in heaven."[23]

"Therefore take care how you listen." [24]

"Beware, and be on your guard against every form of greed."[25]

"Be on guard, that your hearts may not be weighted down with dissipation and drunkenness and the worries of life."[26]

"Let not your heart be troubled; believe in God, believe also in Me."[27]

"Remember the word that I said to you, . . . If they persecuted Me, they will also persecute you."[28]

On one occasion Jesus was very tired. He had been teaching in the Temple all day. The Pharisees, Sadducees, and the scribes had all verbally challenged Him through the day:

"Teacher, we know that you are brutally honest."

"Tell us, should we pay government taxes?"

"Teacher, how do You reconcile marriage and the resurrection?"

"Which Commandment is more important?"[28]

Now Jesus sat down opposite the treasury and watched the multitudes putting money into the offering box. Oh how the people were impressed by large sums of money! Then a poor widow came and put in two copper coins, which make a penny—not enough for anyone to notice except Jesus. He was touched. He knew what those two coins represented to the poor woman. He called the disciples over. "Did you notice," He said, "this poor widow has put in more than all those who are contributing to the treasury"?[30]

Their mouths fell open. *What do you suppose He is talking about this time?* they thought. Jesus wanted His disciples to see true value, real consecration, and God-recognized generosity. Jesus was very conscious of the intent behind actions, the basic drives that prompt human actions. If His disciples could recognize what God required of His followers, and what pleased God, perhaps they would then be able to put things in the right perspective.

Notes

1. Luke 8:42
2. Matthew 9:9
3. Matt. 9:18
4. Luke 6:1
5. Luke 8:49
6. Luke 9:18
7. Mark 7:24
8. Mark 2:1-2a
9. Mark 3:20
10. Luke 4:42
11. Luke 12:1, RSV
12. Mark 3:7-9
13. Matt. 13:1-2, RSV; 14:13-14
14. Matthew 15:10, RSV (author's italics); 15:30; 15:32
15. Matthew 17:9-14, RSV
16. Matthew 20:29-31 (author's italics)
17. Mark 7:24
18. Mark 6:31
19. Mark 6:48-50, RSV
20. Mark 4:34 (author's italics)
21. Mark 8:17, RSV (author's italics)
22. Mark 13:5 (author's italics); 13:9; 13:23; 8:15; 4:24; 13:33; 13:11,13
23. Matthew 6:1 (author's italics); 13:10
24. Luke 8:18 (author's italics); 11:35
25. Luke 12:15 (author's italics); 17:3-4
26. Luke 21:34 (author's italics)
27. John 14:1 (author's italics)
28. John 15:20 (author's italics); 16:1-2; 15:18, GNB; Matthew 15:16; Mark 8:17-18; Mark 8:21; 9:32; 10:24-26
29. Mark 12:14,18,28 (author's paraphrase)
30. Mark 12:41-44, RSV

8

Persons, Not Things

In return for my love they act as my accusers (Ps. 109:4).
If this man were a prophet He would know who and what sort of person
this woman is . . . she is a sinner. (Luke 7:39).

Jesus did not live in a completely masculine society. Although He had male companions, friends, and followers, He also had the constant companionship of women. Jesus exalted the work and place of women. He knew women of all types: graceful women, bossy women, wheedling women, women of charm and beauty, women of means, women who threw themselves at His feet, women with bad reputations, and women with godly reputations.

He recognized many of their problems, and in His special way, He defended and elevated their position in a predominately masculine world. Jesus did not avoid "certain kinds" of women, nor did He make a special effort to please women. He regarded them as individuals worthy of consideration, respect, and love. Not many of the women in the life of Jesus have their names recorded, but we know they were there ministering, supporting with material means and perhaps, some of them thinking in terms of marriage. Jesus saw all women as children of God who had the right to know God the Father. He did not feel bound by the traditional approach to the status of women.

Women were a part of the whole of Jesus' life. They were present at His birth, dedication,[8] early ministry,[2] hours of rest and recreation,[3] later ministry,[4] trial,[5] death,[6] burial,[7] immediately after the resurrection,[8] and following His ascension.[9] Women ministered to Jesus,[10] listened to Him,[11] annoyed Him,[12] and adored him.[13]

Had Jesus desired a married life with children or a life of impurity or immorality, the women were there in adulation, falling at His feet, wanting to demonstrate their love and dedication.[14] At one time or another He had contact with a known "sinner,"[15] an adulteress,[16] and a woman filled with seven evil spirits.[17] It is not impossible or improbable to believe that one or more of the women saw in Jesus more than a prophet or great teacher. Jesus was masculine, dynamic, and assertive. At the same time, He could be tender, kind, and compassionate. Any pastor or Christian counselor can confirm the fact that some women who come in for serious counseling have difficulty in seeing the spiritual person and hearing the spiritual counsel. They are sometimes sidetracked by the physical presence of the counselor.

Jesus was exceptional in His world. He did not downgrade women but treated them as people of worth. To a woman Jesus first announced, "I am the resurrection, and the life: he that believeth in me, though he were dead, yet shall he live."[18] even though she berated Him for having arrived too late to save her brother from death. This same woman, Martha, tried to tell Jesus what to do on two occasions. In the same experience of raising Lazarus from death, Jesus had asked that the stone be removed from the grave where Lazarus was buried, but Martha said to Him, "Lord, by this time there will be a stench; for he has been dead four days." Jesus had to call her hand: "Did I not say to you, if you believe, you will see the glory of God?"

Martha was a take-over woman and Jesus was not immune to her attempts at direction and management. Another time Jesus was visiting the home of Martha and Mary. Mary sat at Jesus' feet, hanging on His every word. Martha, feeling belittled and mistreated because of the work left to her, went to Jesus to complain: "Lord, do You not care that my sister has left me to do all the serving alone? Then tell her to help me."[19]

Jesus did not scold Mary for not helping; He childed Martha: "Martha, Martha, you are worried and bothered about so many things; but only a few things are necessary, really only one, for Mary

has chosen the good part, which shall not be taken away from her."
Did Jesus sense jealousy or possessiveness on Martha's part—resentment that Mary was receiving more attention, had more time to be with Him, or was physically closer to Him? If so, Jesus ignored or sidestepped the issue by defending Mary's desire to hear more of His teachings and experiences.

Once Jesus was resting at the well at Sychar while the disciples went into the village to buy food. A woman of bad reputation came to draw water. She had arrived in the heat of the day, perhaps to avoid the insults and snobbery of the women of the city. Jesus, knowing who she was and what she was, engaged her in a conversation about God and worship. He did not censure her although He let her know that He knew her marital situation. When the disciples came back, "they marveled that He had been speaking with a woman; yet no one said, 'What do You seek?' or 'Why do you speak with her?' "[20]

Jesus did not avoid questionable women, but He did let them know from the beginning that His interest was spiritual. He was not distracted by small talk or chitchat. For this reason the woman returned to the city proclaiming:

> Come, see a man who told me all the things that I have done; this is not the Christ, is it? . . . And from that city many of the Samaritans believed in Him because of the word of the woman who testified.[21]

Jesus was criticized by His disciples and some religious leaders because He let a "sinful woman" anoint His feet: "If this man were a prophet, he would have known who and what sort of woman this is who is touching him, for she is a sinner."[22]

Oh, yes! There were those of the religious hierarchy who kept a careful watch on Jesus' life.

Jesus did not endorse double standards. When the woman taken in adultery was brought before Him, He did not condemn her. Rather He saved her life because she should have been stoned according to the old Mosaic law. How eyebrows must have been raised that Jesus would dare to counsel an adulteress. Jesus cautioned the woman against continuing to sin. How the tongues must have wagged that the Prophet took the side of a sinner against the religious authorities.[23]

Jesus did not avoid the subject of women. He had a healthy attitude toward them in that he could refer to them in illustrations and parables without hesitancy. In His parables and stories He mentioned the ten foolish and the ten wise maidens,[24] two women grinding at the mill,[25] the woman who lost a coin,[26] the woman with leaven[27] and the woman with seven husbands.[28] He did not avoid talking of marriage and the home. Jesus spoke openly and freely of marriage as a natural act of life; He attended a wedding with his mother and performed His first miracle on that occasion. He spoke against adultery, divorce, a house being divided against itself, and in favor of love and care for little children.

Jesus knew the danger of sex sins and warned His followers against them:

> For from within, out of the heart of men, proceed the evil thoughts, and fornications, thefts, murders, adulteries, deeds of coveting and wickedness, as well as deceit, sensuality, envy, slander, pride and foolishness. All these evil things proceed from within and defile the man.[29]

Jesus knew that desire itself can be sinful. Wrong thoughts can/may lead to sinful acts. He did not mince words about the seriousness of sex sins: "For out of the heart come evil thoughts, murders, adulteries, fornications, thefts, false witness, slanders. *These are the things which defile the man.*"[30]

Jesus did not endorse the "new morality" which says that impure thoughts and sexual fantasies are all right and many times healthy. He admonished His followers to keep their thoughts pure and holy and warned them: "But I say to you, that every one who looks on a woman to lust for her has committed adultery with her already in his heart."[31]

Knowing these facts, Jesus fortified Himself to keep His purity. He controlled His thoughts, filled His mind with the Holy Scriptures, communicated with His Heavenly Father often, and kept alive a concern for others.

Notes

1. Luke 2:36-38
2. Mark 1:31
3. Luke 10:38-41
4. Mark 5:24-34
5. Mark 14:66,67,69
6. Luke 23:27
7. Luke 23:55
8. Mark 16:1
9. Acts 1:14
10. Matthew 27:55
11. Luke 10:39
12. Mark 7:26
13. Luke 7:38
14. Luke 8:2-3; John 12:3
15. Luke 7:37
17. Luke 8:2

18. John 11:25, KJV; 11:39-40, NASB
19. Luke 10:38-40, 41-42
20. John 4:27
21. John 4:29,39
22. Luke 7:39, RSV
23. John 8:3-11
24. Matthew 25:1
25. Luke 17:35
26. Luke 15:8
27. Matthew 13:33
28. John 4:7
29. Mark 7:21
30. Matthew 15:19 (author's italics)
31. Matthew 5:28-32

9

Abused, Accused, Misused

He was pierced through for our transgressions (Isa. 53:5).
They kept beating His head with a reed, and spitting at Him (Mark 15:19).

Today we hear much about abuse: child abuse, woman abuse, man abuse, verbal abuse, physical abuse, and mental abuse. Jesus also lived in a violent world and was subjected to mistreatment. Jesus was abused, accused, and misused.

Mental and verbal abuse began with His family and extended to His disciples, religious authorities, and civil authorities.

In the early part of His ministry, when His family should have been supportive and encouraging as Jesus broke away from the tradition of carrying on His profession, we find this story:

> Then Jesus went home. Again such a large crowd gathered that Jesus
> and his disciples had no time to eat. When his family heard about it,
> they set out to take charge of him, because people were saying, "He's
> gone mad!"[1]

Matters were no better at the end of His three-year ministry. His brothers were still resentful and caustic as Jesus went about Galilee and was working His way toward Jerusalem.

There was no hometown pride and honor when Jesus returned to Nazareth for a visit after His many miracles and messages:

> Coming to His hometown He began teaching them in their synagogue,
> so that they became astonished, and said, "Where did this man get this
> wisdom, and these miraculous powers? Is not this the carpenter's son?
> Is not His mother called Mary, and His brothers, James and Joseph and

Simon and Judas? And His sisters, are they not all with us? Where then did this man get all these things?" And they took offense at Him . . . And He did not do many miracles there because of their unbelief.[2]

Oh, the heartbreak of rejection! Jesus surely felt the sting and put-down of his friends and relatives.

The Pharisees and scribes once came to Jesus and asked Him if He was aware that the disciples were breaking tradition. Jesus immediately and openly defended His disciples. Afterwards: "The disciples came and said to him, 'Do you know that the Pharisees were offended when they heard this saying?' "[3] Certainly this was mental abuse. There was no word of gratitude or appreciation for the support of the Master, only criticism because Jesus had offended the very ones that were criticizing *them*. Jesus' own followers chose to bow to the criticism of the Jewish religious leaders rather than show solidarity with Jesus. Was it fear?

Although there was praise, adulation, popularity, and a teeming following, Jesus was never free from the barbs and criticisms of those less captivated by His message and His works. He was accused of being a Samaritan and having a demon.

Once He was asked to identify Himself. It was implied that Jesus had overestimated His personal worth. "Surely You are not greater than our father Abraham, who died? The prophets died too; whom do You make Yourself out to be?"[4]

Another time when Jesus let them know He was aware they wanted to kill Him; they answered, "You have a demon! Who seeks to kill You?"[5]

Jesus was persecuted incessantly and many sought to kill Him. He had just healed a man on the Sabbath. The man told the Jews that Jesus had healed him:

For this reason the Jews were persecuting Jesus, because He was doing these things on the Sabbath. . . . For this cause therefore the Jews were seeking all the more to kill Him, because He not only was breaking the

Sabbath, but also was calling God His own Father, making Himself equal with God.[6]

Jesus healed a man possessed with a multitude of demons. A man who was once violent and uncontrollable became a man who was "clothed and in his right mind." Did the townspeople applaud and honor Him? "Those who had seen it told the people what had happened to the man with the demons, and about the pigs. So they asked Jesus to leave this territory."[7]

When Jesus was mentally agonizing about His approaching death, He begged His closest friends (disciples) to stand by and undergird Him with their prayer support.

> He took with Him Peter and James and John, and began to be very distressed and troubled. And He said to them, "My soul is deeply grieved to the point of death; remain here and keep watch." And He went a little beyond them, and fell to the ground, and began praying that if it were possible, the hour might pass Him by. . . . And He came and found them sleeping, and said to Peter, "Simon, are you asleep? Could you not keep watch for one hour?" . . . And again He went away . . . And again He came and found them sleeping, . . . And He came the third time, and said to them, "Are you still sleeping and taking your rest?"[8]

Jesus wanted the reassurance of those He loved in this final hour of preparation for His crucifixion. After emphasizing the need for their support, He returned twice to see if they were standing by Him. They slept through it all. Then it was too late.

Jesus was surrounded by mental and verbal abuse as He was being prepared for and during His crucifixion. He was aware that He faced physical danger and took steps to avoid danger until the time was right for carrying out His purpose and plan for the salvation of the souls of humankind.

> So from that day on they planned together to kill Him. Jesus therefore no longer continued to walk publicly among the Jews, but went away

from there to the country near the wilderness, into a city called
Ephraim; and there He stayed with the disciples.[9]

Both mental and physical abuse was heaped upon Jesus at His arrest,
His trial, and His crucifixion.

A. From His disciples:
    1. Sleeping instead of praying
    2. Abandonment when He was taken prisoner
    3. Peter's denial
    4. Judas's betrayal

B. From the Jewish religious leaders and people:
    1. Mock trial
    2. "Then *they spat in his face* and *struck him with their fists;*
        and others said, as *they beat him,* 'Now, Messiah, if you
        are a prophet, tell us who hit you.' "[10]
    3. "When morning came, the chief priests and the elders of
        the nation met in conference to *plan the death of Jesus.
        They then put him in chains* and led him away, to hand
        him over to Pilate the Roman Governor."[11]
    4. When before Pilate: "For he knew that *it was out of malice*
        that they had brought Jesus before him."[12]
    5. "Meanwhile the chief priests and elders had *persuaded the
        crowd* to ask for the release of Bar-Abbas and *to have
        Jesus put to death.*"[13]
    6. " 'Then what am I to do with Jesus called Messiah?' asked
        Pilate; and *with one voice they answered, 'Crucify him!'*
        "Why, what harm has he done?' Pilate asked; but *they
        shouted all the louder, 'Crucify him!'* "[14]
    7. "So also the chief priests *mocked him to one another* with
        the scribes saying, 'He saved others; he cannot save him-
        self. Let the the Christ, the King of Israel, come down
        now from the cross, that we may see and believe.' "[15]

C. From the civil authorities:

1. "Whereupon Pilate . . . had Jesus *flogged* and handed over for crucifixion."[16]

2. "Then Pilate's soldiers took Jesus into the governor's palace, and the whole company gathered around him. *They stripped off his clothes* and put a scarlet robe on him."[17]

3. "Then *they made a crown out of thorny branches and placed it on his head,* and put a stick in his right hand; then they knelt before him and *made fun of him.* 'Long live the King of the Jews!' they said."[18]

4. *"They spat on him,* and *took the stick and hit him over the head."*[19]

5. "When they had finished *making fun of him,* they took the robe off and put his own clothes back on him. Then *they led him out to crucify him."*[20]

6. "When they came to a place called Golgotha . . . *they offered him wine to drink, mingled with gall."*[21]

7. "They crucified him, and divided his garments among them, casting lots for them, to decide what each should take."[22]

Through the ordeal of the trial and mockery of the troops, Jesus had been so abused that He was physically unable to carry His cross to Calvary. The soldiers pressed another man, Simon of Cyrene, into the service of carrying His cross.

D. From those passing by and the spectators:

1. *"Those who passed by hurled insults at him, shaking their heads* and saying, 'You who are going to destroy the temple and build it in three days, save yourself! Come down from the cross, if you are the Son of God.' "[23]

2. "Some of the people standing there heard him and said, 'He is calling for Elijah!' One of them ran up at once, took

a sponge, soaked it in cheap wine, put it on the end of a stick, and tried to make him drink it. But the others said, 'Wait, let us see if Elijah is coming to save him!' "[24]

E.   From the robbers crucified with him:

1.   *"One of the criminals hanging there hurled insults at him:* 'Aren't you the Messiah? Save yourself and us!' "[25]

Perhaps the greatest suffering of all that Jesus bore came upon Him not because He was Jesus but because He was the "scapegoat," wearing and bearing the evil and wicked sins of the world. "At about three o'clock Jesus cried out with a loud shout, *'Eli, Eli, lema sabachthani?'* which means, 'My God, my God, why did you abandon me?' "[26]

If you have any problems in your life related to abuse in any form, you have a perfect Comforter, One who understands all kinds of torment, mistreatment, and physical violence. Jesus, from the time He initiated His ministry until His death, suffered untold hate, violence, and persecution.

Notes

1. Mark 3:20-21, GNB

2. Matthew 13:54-58

3. Matthew 15:12, RSV

4. John 8:53

5. John 7:19-20

6. John 5:16-18

7. Mark 5:16, GNB

8. Mark 14:33-38

9. John 11:53-54; 10:39, RSV; 7:1; 8:59

10. Matthew 26:67, NEB (author's italics)

11. Matthew 27:1-2 NEB (author's italics)

12. Matthew 27:18, NEB (author's italics)

13. Matthew 27:20, NEB (author's italics)

14. Matthew 27:22-23, NEB (author's italics)

15. Mark 15:31-32, RSV (author's italics)

16. Matthew 27:26, Phillips (author's italics)

17. Matthew 27:27-28, GNB (author's italics)

18. Matthew 27:29, GNB (author's italics)

19. Matthew 27:30, GNB (author's italics)

20. Matthew 27:31, GNB (author's italics)

21. Matthew 27:33*b*-34*a*, RSV (author's italics)

22. Mark 15:24, RSV

23. Matthew 27:39-40, NIV (author's italics)

24. Matthew 27:47-49, GNB (author's italics)

25. Luke 23:39, GNB (author's italics)

26. Matthew 27:46, GNB (author's italics)

10

Personnel Problems!

He . . . chose twelve of them, whom He also named as apostles (Luke 6:13).

Jesus knows what it is like to be "used" by one's friends and colleagues. Never has anyone had a more unlikely or dissimilar group of co-workers. Jesus, by profession, was a carpenter. Four of His disciples were fishermen. There was also a tax collector and one man with a talent for handling money. There were two sets of brothers. Among the disciples there were:

1. Men with Volatile Personalities—James and John: Whom Jesus nicknamed Boanerges or "Sons of Thunder."[1]
2. A Thief—Judas: "Not that he cared for the poor but because he was a thief, and as he had the money box he used to take what was put into it."[2]
3. A Betrayer—Judas: He said to the chief priests, "What will you give me if I deliver him to you?"[3]
4. A Doubter—Thomas: He said, "Unless I see in his hands the print of the nails, and place my finger in the mark of the nails, and place my hand in his side, I will not believe."[4]
5. A Man Who Used Bad Language—Peter: He "again denied it with an oath . . . Then he began to invoke a curse on himself."[5]
6. A Braggart—Peter: with a great sense of self-importance declared, " 'Though they all fall away because of you, I will never fall away.' Jesus said to him, 'Truly, I say to you, this very night, before the cock crows, you will deny me three times.'

Peter said to him, 'Even if I must die with you, I will not deny you.' "[6]

7. A Patriot and Nationalist—Simon: "Simon the Cananaean" or "Simon who was called the Zealot."[7]

8. An Overzealous Big Mouth—Peter: At the transfiguration Peter said, "It is well that we are here; if you wish, I will make three booths here, one for you and one for Moses and one for Elijah."[8] "For he did not know what to say."[9]

9. A Man who was Enthusiastic but Exasperating—Peter: "Peter replied, 'You are the Christ, the Son of the living God.' . . . And Peter took him and began to rebuke him, saying, 'God forbid, Lord! This shall never happen to you.' "[10]

10. A Man who Denied Knowing Him—Peter: Peter denied knowing Jesus three times. "Woman, I do not know Him."[11]

11. A Possible Foreigner—Philip (a Greek name): "Now among those who went up to worship at the feast were some Greeks. So these came to Philip, who was from Bethsaida in Galilee."[12]

12. A Man Who Collaborated with a Foreign Government—Matthew: "As Jesus passed on from there, He saw a man, called Matthew, sitting in the tax office; and He said to him, 'Follow me!' And he rose and followed Him."[13]

13. A Man Whose Mother Was Often Close By—James the son of Alphaeus! "Mary the mother of James the younger . . . who, when he was in Galilee, followed him, and ministered to him."[14] This was not necessarily a problem, but it would undoubtedly have had some influence, good or bad, on the relationship.

14. A Man of Responsibility—Andrew: "One of the two who heard John speak, and followed him, was Andrew, Simon Peter's brother. He found first his own brother Simon."[15] "Philip came and told Andrew; Andrew and Philip came, and they told Jesus."[16]

"One of his disciples, Andrew, . . . said to Him, 'There is a lad here, who has five barley loaves and two fish.' "[17]

15. Men Who Were Ambitious—James and John: "Then the mother of the sons of Zebedee came up to him, with her sons, . . . 'Command that these two sons of mine may sit, one at your right hand and one at your left, in your kingdom.' But Jesus answered, 'You do not know what you are asking. Are you able to drink the cup that I am to drink? They said to him, 'We are able.' "[18]

16. A Man with Social Standing—John: "This disciple was known to the high priest."[19]

17. One Who Didn't Seem to Know What Was Going On—Philip: "Jesus said to Philip, 'How are we to buy bread, so that these people may eat? This he said to test him, . . . Philip answered him, 'Two hundred denarii would not buy enough bread for each of them to get a little.' "[20]

"If you had known me, you would have known my Father also; henceforth you know him and have seen him. Philip said to him, 'Lord, show us the Father, and we shall be satisfied.' Jesus said to him, 'Have I been with you so long, and yet you do not know me, Philip?' "[21]

18. A Man Who Was Sincere—Nathanael: "When Jesus saw Nathanael coming, he said, 'Here is an Israelite worthy of the name; there is nothing false in Him.' "[22]

19. A Man Willing to Face Any Danger with Jesus—Thomas: "Thomas, called the Twin, said to his fellow disciples, 'Let us also go, that we may die with him.' "[23]

20. A Man Who Could Not Understand the Spiritual Kingdom of Jesus:—"Judas (not Iscariot): said to Him, 'Lord, what then has happened that You are going to disclose Yourself to us, and not to the world?"[24]

21. Men Who Were Jealous of Each Other:—"They began to discuss among themselves which one of them it might be who

was going to do this thing. And there arose also a dispute among them as to which one of them was regarded to be greatest."[25]

It isn't easy to work with others and put up with their self-centered attitudes, their pettiness, their provocations, and their callousness. The personalities and characteristics found in Jesus' helpers are the same we find in people today. Some of our co-workers have a combination of undesirable qualities, like the disciples, that make life miserable and irritating. Jesus sought to deal with the basic person because He saw the inherent worth in each individual in spite of the outward manifestations. Oh, how they vexed Him and tried His patience. But Jesus never let them make Him forget who He was and for whom He was working. He did not let them make Him sin.

Jesus knew that one day He would die for his co-workers. It did not stop Him from going ahead with His plans even though His own helpers bickered, criticized, disbelieved, abandoned, and didn't understand Him.

"Having loved His own who were in the world, He loved them to the end."[26]

Notes

1. Mark 3:17
2. John 12:6, RSV
3. Matthew 26:15, RSV
4. John 20:25, RSV
5. Matthew 26:72-74, RSV
6. Matthew 26:33-35, RSV
7. Mark 3:18, RSV; Luke 6:15, RSV
8. Matthew 17:4, RSV
9. Mark 9:6, RSV
10. Matthew 16:16-22, RSV
11. Luke 22:57
12. John 12:20-21, RSV
13. Matthew 9:9
14. Mark 15:40, RSV
15. John 1:40-41
16. John 12:22
17. John 6:8-9
18. Matthew 20:20-22, RSV
19. John 18:15, RSV
20. John 6:5, RSV
21. John 14:7-9, RSV
22. John 1:47, NEB
23. John 11:16, RSV
24. John 14:22
25. Luke 22:23-24
26. John 13:1

11

The Pesky Disciples

Come away . . . and rest a while (Mark 6:31).

The disciples had just returned from a preaching mission. Jesus knew that they were tired and suggested that they go with Him to a desert place for a retreat: rest. "Come away by yourselves to a lonely place and rest a while."[1] They climbed into a boat and went to a quiet place.

But the crowds would not be outdone. They noticed the direction which the boat took and rushed "on foot" to the place in order to be there when the boat landed. What a disappointment it must have been to the disciples who had returned from their successful mission tour, happy but tired, enthusiastic about the results—full of news and wanting to tell Jesus. They had welcomed the idea of a quiet rest.

The disciples put up with the crowd until evening came. "Since it is getting late, and this is a lonely place, send the people away," they urged. Jesus sensed they were miffed so He suggested, perhaps with a bit of teasing, "You give them something to eat!" Their answer was anything but congenial, "Shall we go and buy two hundred dollars' worth of bread, and give it to them to eat?" As tired as they were, surely Jesus didn't expect *them* to go all the way into the towns to buy the food! The expense was prohibitive.

Jesus pretended He didn't notice their sarcasm and resentment. "How about going and finding out how much food we have available among the crowd?" The disciples returned with the report. "Five loaves and two fish," they answered.

72

"Then let's divide the crowd into groups of fifty and one hundred," Jesus suggested. After a prayer of thanksgiving, Jesus began to divide the bread and fish and guess who served the crowds![2] That wasn't all. There were twelve baskets full of broken pieces to gather up afterwards.

Then Jesus, with love, told His disciples that they must get in the boat and leave, and He would take care of the closing service, I think they left unhappy. Mark says that "He made his disciples get into the boat and go before Him."[3]

I suspect that the further they rowed, the more resentful they became. Then the wind rose against them, and they were distressed in rowing. Remember that these were experienced fishermen accustomed to storms.

Jesus came walking toward them on the water somewhere between three and six o'clock in the morning. When the disciples saw Him, they were terrified. Immediately, Jesus identified Himself and got into the boat. And here we have an interesting statement:

> He got into the boat with them, and the wind stopped; and they were greatly astonished, for they had not gained any insight from the incident of the loaves, but their heart was hardened.[4]

They were angry with Jesus and the way He had handled the whole situation since their victorious return.

The disciples were proud of their accomplishments: they wanted to brag to Jesus about what they had done—tell their experiences. When the crowds caught up with them, Jesus felt the greater responsibility of ministering to the needs of the people. His disciples needed a rest. *He* needed a rest. But the people needed more: they needed healing for their bodies and food for their souls. The greater necessity must be cared for first. Jesus calmly set about doing what He had to do.

They Get on My Nerves!

So send the multitudes away (Matt. 14:15).

How many leaders could hold a group together for very long if the members were as contentious as the disciples? We have very few accounts in the Gospels of their complete support, their comprehension and acceptance of Jesus and His cause.

Many times they seemed to have completely missed the mark. Organization for organization's sake; put up with the crowds, but don't make a fetish of them; do what you can, but don't get uptight about not getting around to everything you want to do; "hang loose" —this seemed to be the general attitude of the disciples. Do what Jesus says, but no more.

Even then they were known to grumble and complain. They had difficulty in understanding Jesus' teachings. They had trouble accepting His habits: going out alone to pray at all hours of the day and night, seeking out the crowds, loving little children, treating women as well as He treated the men. They felt He definitely needed orientation—someone to help Him with the priorities and program of work. Here are a few examples.

After feeding the five thousand, Jesus and the disciples traveled and worked. Then once again, a large crowd had been with Him for several days, and Jesus was concerned about them. Isn't it entirely plausible that Jesus decided to test His disciples and give them another chance to respond in love to a known situation? For the Bible tells us:

> Jesus summoned to Himself His disciples, and said, "I feel compassion for the multitude, because they have remained with Me now three days and have nothing to eat; and I do not wish to send them away hungry, lest they faint on the way." And the disciples said to Him, "Where would we get so many loaves in a desolate place to satisfy such a great multitude."[5]

I think Jesus may have paused just a moment before He asked, "How many loaves do you have?" They said, "Seven, and a few small fish." They had remembered the last time when Jesus sent them to search out food from among the crowd. They already had the answer ready for Him. Why didn't they immediately say, "Don't worry. We have seven loaves of bread and a few small fish, and You can do what You did the last time"? But they resented the crowd and the task they were assigned to do. Jesus took the bread and fish and "having given thanks he broke them and gave them to the disciples, and the disciples gave them to the crowds."[6]

His disciples enjoyed the position but didn't think much of the work. At the feeding of the five thousand when evening came, the disciples took the initiative. "The disciples came to him and said, 'This is a lonely place, and the day is now over; send the crowds away.' "[7]

Then the disciples wanted to send the children away:

Some people brought children to Jesus for him to touch them, but the disciples scolded those people. When Jesus noticed it, he was angry and said to his disciples, "Let the children come to me, and do not stop them."[8]

The disciples did not care to be bothered by foreigners:

Jesus went away from there, and withdrew into the district of Tyre and Sidon. And behold, a Canaanite woman came out from that region, and began to cry out, saying, "Have mercy on me, O Lord, Son of David; my daughter is cruelly demon-possessed." But He did not answer her a word. And His disciples came to Him and kept asking Him, saying, 'Send her away, for she is shouting out after *us*.'[9]

On another occasion the disciples left Jesus at a well while they went into the nearby "foreign" town to buy food. When they returned, Jesus was talking to a Samaritan woman: "At this point His disciples came, and they marveled that He had been speaking with a woman."[10]

Jesus' friends and co-workers REBUKED Him: Jesus had just

defended His disciples from an attack by the Pharisees. His disciples became concerned: 'Do You know that the Pharisees were offended when they heard this statement?"[11] Again, Peter had just made his great affirmation, "Thou art the Christ, the Son of the living God," when Jesus confided to His disciples what the future held for Him:

> From that time Jesus Christ began to show His disciples that He must go to Jerusalem, and suffer many things from the elders and chief priests and scribes, and be killed, and be raised up on the third day. And Peter took Him aside and began to rebuke Him, saying, "God forbid it, Lord! This shall never happen to You."[12]

His disciples and followers *tried to direct His life and tell Him what to do.*

> In the early morning, while it was still dark, He arose and went out and departed to a lonely place, and was praying there. And Simon and his companions hunted for Him; and they found Him, and said to Him, "Everyone is looking for You."[13]

> When day came, He departed and went to a lonely place; and the multitudes were searching for Him, and came to Him, and tried to keep Him from going away from them."[14]

The disciples *questioned His methods:* "The disciples came and said to Him, 'Why do You speak to them in parables?"[15]

The disciples *argued and became angry with each other.*

> Then the mother of the sons of Zebedee came to Him . . . "Command that in Your kingdom these two sons of mine may sit, one on Your right and one on Your left." . . . And hearing this, the ten became indignant at the two brothers."[16]

We dislike being used. We rebel when we feel people are with us because of what they can get out of us. We resent it when the people who are with us try to manipulate us, run our lives, or tell us what to do because they don't think we are handling things correctly or we don't have the know-how to do things. Jesus faced it all. He knew what He was doing. He knew what His purpose in life was, and He refused to sin by striking back at those who were constantly calling His attention to what He was or was not doing.

What's in It for Me?

What then will there be for us? (Matt. 19:27).

All of Jesus' trials and tribulations happened over a brief period of thirty-three years. He felt problems and pressures with an intensity and concentration unknown to the rest of humankind. Those problems dealing with family and neighbors covered the entire period of His life. The relationships with the public and especially His disciples occurred over a period of just three brief years.

What did the disciples want from and with Jesus? We can only surmise about certain, but the Bible gives us information of some specific goals they had:

1. *They wanted positions.* Twice we have accounts of of the disciples arguing about who would be in first place:

When he was in the house he asked them, "What were you discussing on the way?" But they were silent; for on the way they had discussed with one another who was the greatest.[17]

Even at the Passover supper, the last supper with Jesus, an incident happened which leaves us amazed:

Then a jealous dispute broke out: who among them should rank highest?[18]

Once, two of the disciples asked their mother to intercede for them and ask for the best places in the Kingdom.

The mother of Zebedee's sons then came before him, with her sons. She bowed low and begged a favour. "What is it you wish?" asked Jesus. "I want you," she said, "to give orders that in your kingdom my two sons here may sit next to you, one at your right, and the other at your left."

Jesus knew where the interest and desire had come from because He turned to the two disciples and asked, "Can you drink the cup that I am to drink?"[19]

2.   *The disciples wanted power.* When Jesus started back to Jerusalem, He sent some messengers ahead to a Samaritan village to make arrangements for Him to stay there.

And they did not receive Him, because He was journeying with His face toward Jerusalem. And when His disciples James and John saw this, they said, "Lord, do you want us to command fire to come down from heaven and consume them?"[20]

> Another time "the seventy returned with joy, saying, 'Lord, even the demons are subject to us in your name.' "[21]

Once Jesus

called to him the twelve, and began to send them out two by two, and gave them authority over the unclean spirits. . . . So they went out and preached that men should repent. And they cast out many demons, and anointed with oil many that were sick and healed them. . . . The apostles returned to Jesus, and told him all that they had done and taught.[22]

> On another occasion, the disciples tried to use the power by themselves and failed. Jesus had been on the Mount of Transfiguration with Peter, James, and John. After the marvelous experience of the transfiguration they came down to join the other disciples.

And when they came back to the disciples, they saw a large crowd around them, and some scribes arguing with them. . . . And He asked them, "What are you discussing with them?" And one of the crowd answered Him, "Teacher, I brought You my son, . . . And I told Your disciples to cast it out, and they could not do it."

Later, when

He had come into the house, His disciples began questioning Him privately, "Why is it that we could not cast it out?"[23]

3. *The disciples wanted personal privilege.* Once again we look at the incident when the mother of James and John came with a request that her two sons be allowed to have the best seats—those on either side of Jesus when He came into His kingdom. After all, weren't her two sons closer to Jesus than the other disciples? Didn't Jesus include them in more events, and weren't they in the "inner circle"?

> When Peter and the other disciples were with Jesus, and He told them how hard it was for the more affluent people to enter the kingdom of heaven, they were disturbed and implored, "We have left everything and followed you. What will that be worth to us?"[24]

4. I think we can rightly assume that *the disciples were interested in possessions:*
    Once a scribe

came and said to Him, "Teacher, I will follow You wherever You go." And Jesus said to him, "The foxes have holes, and the birds of the air have nests; but the Son of Man has nowhere to lay His head."[25]

> Then we can cite the same passage above when Peter asked the question that probably everyone of the disciples had thought about and perhaps discussed with one another: "We left everything to follow you. What will we get out of it?"[26]

Perhaps we wonder why Jesus didn't get rid of the whole group. He well realized what they were, what they wanted, and what their weaknesses were. But He also knew that: "All we like sheep have gone astray; we have turned everyone to his own way; and the Lord has laid on him [Jesus] the iniquity of us all."[27] THAT was the purpose of His coming.

In spite of their secondary purposes in following Him, in spite of their insults and sarcasm, in spite of their bickering, He loved them. He made allowances for them, and He defended them from outward attacks. He saw in them a potential for something higher and nobler. He saw what they could be with the love of His Father. He accepted them as they were and gave them the opportunity to improve and learn. And He did not let their attitudes and actions lower Him to their level.

I Didn't Hear You

Remember how He spoke to you (Luke 24:6).

Jesus advised the disciples many times that He was going to die and be raised from the dead.

> From that time Jesus Christ began to show His disciples that He must go to Jerusalem, and suffer many things from the elders and chief priests and scribes, and be killed, *and be raised up on the third day.*[28]

Although Jesus was well aware of the type of death He was going to have, the suffering that was awaiting Him, He did not "go to pieces" or become desperate. He did not try to run from His problem or pamper Himself to prepare for the ordeal.

> After singing a hymn, they went out to the Mount of Olives. And Jesus said to them, "You will all fall away, because it is written, 'I will strike down the shepherd, and the sheep shall be scattered.' But after I have been raised, I will go before you to *Galilee.*"[29]

The disciples were all together in the upper room with many other followers of Jesus. There were sad but excited. There were only two days left to get everything done. Well, really there was only one day—the sabbath had begun, and they were limited about what they could do, but they could make plans!

Peter assumed the leadership, which seemed only natural at that time. He was speaking, "Now John and I will stay here in Jerusalem, and the rest of you, including the women, will go on up to Galilee as soon as the sabbath is past. There you will prepare the welcome party for Jesus." Peter continued, "Fix all the things He likes, call in His closest friends and followers there in Galilee."

The women, Mary Magdalene and the mother of Jesus included, had stayed with the body of Jesus until He had been laid in the tomb and the rock rolled in place. They could tell Peter and John where to go to meet Jesus.

They were planning a VICTORY RALLY for Jesus, for hadn't He said, "Destroy this temple, and in three days I will raise it up"?[30] And "after I have been raised, I will go before you to Galilee"?[31]

Wouldn't it be wonderful if all of the above story had taken place? Jesus had told His disciples more than once about His coming death, but He had always spoken of His resurrection at the same time.

If the disciples had listened to what Jesus had said, If they had understood, If just one of them had actually taken Jesus seriously when He told them repeatedly about His death and resurrection: Why didn't at least one of them get up early on that Sunday morning to go down to the tomb to wait for Him? If only one of them had said, "You know, Jesus said He would arise the third day and would meet us in Galilee. Let's go on up there and be ready to meet Him." Then they would have left immediately to be there when He arrived, except, of course, for those who would wait at the tomb to accompany Him on the trip.

How sad that the disciples did not hear the words about the resurrection. Worse, they didn't hear the words about His death. They went into a state of shock when Jesus was actually taken, tried, and crucified. They were still thinking in terms of a messiah who would reign right then on earth, and their positions. They didn't hear because they did not want to hear. They did not want to accept Jesus' teaching on the matter. With all the miracles they had seen, all the teaching and preaching they had heard, they were not prepared to remember His words, "After I am raised up, I will go before you to Galilee."[32]

Jesus knew the disciples had not gone into Galilee, as He had told them, for when the angel appeared to the women on that memorable first day of the week and told them to go quickly and inform the disciples that He was risen from the dead, he also promised that Jesus would go before them into Galilee where they would see Him.[33]

> Remember how He told you, while he was still in Galilee, that the Son of man must be delivered into the hands of sinful men, and be crucified, and on the third day rise," And they remembered His words.[34]

It is interesting to note that the enemies of Jesus expected something of the disciples—that they would try to steal the body of Jesus from the tomb.

> The chief priests and the Pharisees gathered together with Pilate, and said, "Sir, we remember that when He was still alive that deceiver said, "After three days I am to rise again." Therefore, give orders for the grave to be made secure until the third day, *lest the disciples come and steal Him away and say to the people, 'He has risen from the dead,'* and the last deception will be worse than the first."[35]

The message that the disciples missed, the Pharisees and the unbelievers heard and acknowledged. They didn't really believe that Jesus would rise from the dead, but *they believed that Jesus said He would rise from the dead.* They expected affirmative action from the disciples. But the disciples missed this glorious message. They were like cowered animals in a room: "The doors were shut where the disciples were, for fear of the Jews."[36]

Yet, we dare not condemn the disciples when we ourselves are guilty of forgetting so many of Jesus' words and commands, guilty of listening without hearing and understanding. We are still hiding in a room afraid of the world and criticism. We still don't understand much of what Jesus did and said. We are timid followers of our Lord. We fret, we worry, we complain, and we become discouraged. We are not satisfied with what we have; we take matters into our own hands because God is not working as quickly as we want Him to work. We don't hear what Jesus actually said, but we, like His former disciples, envision what we would like for Him to have said and meant. We also would not have been at the tomb or in Galilee eagerly awaiting His arrival, for we, too, are of little faith!

Notes

1. Mark 6:30-31
2. Mark 6:41
3. Mark 6:45, RSV
4. Mark 6:51b-52
5. Matthew 15:32-33
6. Matthew 15:34-36, RSV
7. Matthew 14:15, RSV
8. Mark 10:13-14, GNB
9. Matthew 15:21-23
10. John 4:27
11. Matthew 15:12
12. Matthew 16:16-22
13. Mark 1:35-37
14. Luke 4:42
15. Matthew 13:10
16. Matthew 20:20-24
17. Mark 9:33-34, RSV
18. Luke 22:24, NEB
19. Matthew 20:20-22, NEB
20. Luke 9:53-54
21. Luke 10:17
22. Mark 6:7, 12-13, 30, RSV
23. Mark 9:14, 16-18, 28
24. Matthew 19:27, Phillips
25. Matthew 8:19-20
26. Matthew 19:23-27, TLB
27. Isaiah 53:6, RSV
28. Matthew 16:21, 17:9; 17:22;
Mark 10:33-34, RSV
29. Mark 14:26-28
30. John 2:19
31. Mark 14:28
32. Matthew 26:32, RSV
33. Matthew 28:5-7
34. Luke 24:6-8, RSV
35. Matthew 27:62-64
36. John 20:19

12

How Jesus Handled It

All things have been handed over to Me by My Father (Matt. 11:27).

Faith in a Loving Father

Jesus' admiration, devotion, and all-encompassing belief in His Father is evident in His prayers, His teachings, and His actions. God the Father. God the Son. The experience at His baptism, when God publicly confirmed Himself to Jesus as His personal Father, had been reaffirmed on the Mount of Transfiguration. Through His prayers and experiential living, He was more than confident that God was His Father. The depth of this belief was the controlling fulcrum of His life. His Father was perfect; likewise was and is the Son. "Therefore you are to be perfect, as your heavenly Father is perfect.[1]

Jesus' acceptance of humanity, His life of trials, tribulations, temptations, humiliations, and His final acceptance of death on the cross as the only way to secure eternal salvation for His followers were based on His complete faith in God the Father.

In reading the Book of John we find over seventy-five references to Jesus' Father. In the other Gospels, Jesus used the term *Father* fifteen times in prayer. He spoke of:

His Father's Kingdom: "I tell you I shall not drink again of this fruit of the vine until that day when I drink it new with you in my Father's kingdom."[2]

His Father's business: "Wist ye not that I must be about my Father's business?"[3]

His Father's good pleasure: "Do not be afraid, little flock, for your Father has chosen gladly to give you the kingdom."[4]

His Father's name: "I have come in My Father's name."[5]

His Father's house: "In My Father's house are many dwelling places"[6]

His Father's commandments: "Just as I have kept My Father's commandments, and abide in His love."[7]

Although He was surprised and disappointed at the reactions of His followers and the religious leaders, Jesus knew His position with His Father:

> For I did not speak on My own initiative, but the Father Himself who sent Me has given Me commandment, what to say, and what to speak.[8]

> All things have been handed over to Me by My Father; and no one knows the Son, except the Father; nor does anyone know the Father except the Son, and anyone to whom the Son wills to reveal Him.[9]

Like an adoring son who tries to imitate his loving father, so Jesus imitated His Heavenly Father:

> He answered them, "My Father is working until now, and I Myself am working."[10]

> Jesus therefore answered and was saying to them, "Truly, Truly, I say to you, the Son can do nothing of Himself, unless it is something He sees the Father doing; for whatever the Father does, these things the Son also does in like manner. For the Father loves the Son, and shows Him all things that He Himself is doing; and greater works than these will He show Him, that you may marvel."[11]

Through Jesus' love for His Heavenly Father, He so identified with Him that He lived His life here on earth as He believed the Father would have lived.

I glorified Thee on the earth, having accomplished the work which
Thou hast given Me to do. . . . I manifested Thy name to the men whom
Thou gavest Me out of the world; Thine they were, and Thou gavest
them to Me, . . . Now they have come to know that everything Thou
hast given Me is from Thee; for the words which Thou gavest Me I have
given to them; . . . all things that are Mine are Thine, and Thine are
Mine.[12]

Although Jesus was the only begotten Son of the Father, His honor
and glory did not come from a privileged life.

In the days of His flesh, He offered up both prayers and supplications
with loud crying and tears to the One able to save Him from death, and
He was heard because of His piety. Although He was a Son, He learned
obedience from the things which He suffered.[13]

By Jesus' own word, we who are born again are coheirs with Him
and can have the same confidence and fellowship with the Father.

My sheep hear my voice, and I know them, and they follow me; and
I give them eternal life, and they shall never perish, and no one shall
snatch them out of my hand. My Father, who has given them to me,
is greater than all, and no one is able to snatch them out of the Father's
hand. I and the Father are one."[14]

What a beautiful relationship existed between Jesus and His Father!
The cares of the world could not drag Him down; the criticism and
belittling of His friends and the religious leaders could not defeat him;
the lack of material things did not worry Him; His fellowship and
communion with His loving, caring, supreme Father filled every void
in His life. As He spoke of His experiences with His Father to His
disciples, He wanted to show them that His Father also loved and
would care for them. The Father was available for the asking. Today's
disciples also have the option of asking for and receiving the presence
of the Father and the assurance of His love and concern for us. The

Holy Spirit is ready to live with us and in us to reaffirm over and over again that God the Father loves us and is accessible to us.

Prayer, Prayer, Prayer

He departed to the mountain to pray. (Mark 6:46).

There are many instances in the Bible that tell of Jesus' need for and dedication to prayer. Since He was and is the Son of God, He realized more than anyone else the sheer necessity of keeping communication lines open with God the Father from Whom He was receiving His inspirational, physical, mental, and spiritual force to face the many trials and temptations that assailed Him on every side.

Jesus did not pray the childish: "Now I lay me down to sleep" or "God is great, God is good, Let us thank Him for our food." He agonized in prayer. In Hebrews 5:7 we read:

> In the days of his earthly life he offered up prayers and petitions, with loud cries and tears, to God who was able to deliver him from the grave. Because of his humble submission his prayer was heard: son though he was, he learned obedience in the school of suffering (NEB).

In John 6:15 we read that the crowds wanted to take Jesus by force and make Him their king. What a good time to pray! Jesus realized what the crowds had in mind, and He knew this was not the plan that God had for His life. So He went off "again to the mountain by Himself alone." He took Himself out of the way of temptation. He went away from the escalating problem.

It is natural that the relationship Jesus had with His Heavenly Father would cause Him to seek out His Father at every opportunity. Everyone needs a confidant. Jesus also needed someone with whom He could talk out His problems and the temptations that constantly attacked Him on every side. He needed reassuring and fortifying in the face of criticism, ridicule, scorn, and contempt. He needed extra strength for the heavy demands made upon His time and His physical strength. He learned early that the inner force He needed came from God: His Father. He knew the scrolls of Isaiah and the truth of the words written there:

> Yet those who wait for the Lord/Will gain new strength;/They will mount up with wings like eagles,/They will run and not get tired,/They will walk and not become weary.[15]

Many times the multitudes and disciples couldn't understand why Jesus had to have time alone for prayer.

> In the early morning, while it was still dark, He arose and went out and departed to a lonely place, and was praying there. And Simon and his companions hunted for Him; and they found Him, and said to Him, "Everyone is looking for You."[16]

There are so many references to Jesus' praying. He did not hesitate to leave His disciples to the side and separate Himself for prayer. He was not ashamed for others to see Him praying. "Then Jesus came with them to a place called Gethsemane, and said to His disciples, 'Sit here while I go over there and pray.' "[17]

At times the disciples felt there were great opportunities and that maybe Jesus should leave off His prayer time to care for pressing needs. Many Christians today feel that when the work load is great there is *no time* for prayer and Bible study. Jesus' attitude was exactly the opposite. When the pressures were greatest and time was shortest, He felt His greatest need was prime time with the Father.

Every facet of Jesus' life was bathed in prayer. Before He chose His disciples, He spent the night in prayer.

> It was at this time that He went off to the mountain to pray, and He spent the whole night in prayer to God. And when day came, He called His disciples to Him; and chose twelve of them, whom He also named as apostles.[18]

Jesus set an example of prayer before His disciples. "And it came about that while He was praying alone, the disciples were with Him."[19]

He taught His disciples *how* to pray:

"*When you are praying,* do not use meaningless repetition, as the Gentiles do, for they suppose that they will be heard for their many words. Therefore do not be like them; for your Father knows what you need, before you ask Him. Pray, then, in this way."[20]

Jesus taught His disciples *to* pray.

"But you, *when you pray,* GO INTO YOUR INNER ROOM, AND WHEN YOU HAVE SHUT YOUR DOOR, pray to your Father who is in secret, and your Father who sees in secret will repay you. And *when you are praying,* do not use meaningless repetition."[21]

Jesus taught them *faith* in praying. "Therefore I say to you, all things for which you pray and ask, *believe that you have received them,* and they shall be granted you."[22]

He taught them the *power* of prayer.

I say to you, ask, and it shall be given to you; seek, and you shall find; knock, and it shall be opened to you. For everyone who asks, receives; and he who seeks, finds; and to him who knocks, it shall be opened. ... If you then, being evil, know how to give good gifts to your children, how much more shall your heavenly Father give the Holy Spirit to those who ask Him?[23]

He Had a Complete
Knowledge of the Scriptures

It is written (Matt. 4:4).

When Jesus was twelve years old his parents carried Him to Jerusalem to observe the Passover. After the commemoration it was time to return to Nazareth. Apparently, Jesus was a responsible lad because His parents did not think it necessary to look for Him to be sure He was in the large group of pilgrims going north. They started on the journey assuming that He was with them.[24] Jesus was not aware that the group going to Nazareth had left. He was at the Temple "sitting in the midst of the teachers, both listening to them, and asking them questions."[25]

It wasn't a case of disobedience or rebellion. Jesus had found something that made Him forget the passage of time and the pressure of responsibilities. He had found someone with whom He could exchange ideas and find answers to the many things He did not understand about the Word of God. Jesus was so engrossed in His study that He was not concerned that His parents had been searching for Him. He thought they knew where He would be. Jesus continued this intense interest in God's Word because He not only knew the Scriptures, He also knew how to interpret them.

After Jesus' baptism, He was "led about by the Spirit in the wilderness."[26] When the days of fasting were over, the devil came to tempt Him three times. In all three temptations, Jesus made His decision on the basis of the Scriptures.

> Jesus answered him, "*It is written,* 'Man shall not live on bread alone.' "[27]

> Jesus answered and said to him, "*It is written,* 'You shall worship the Lord your God and serve Him only.' "

After failing on the first two attempts, Satan very astutely tempted Jesus using the Scriptures also.

> He led Him to Jerusalem and set Him on the pinnacle of the temple, and said to Him, "If you are the Son of God, cast Yourself down from here; *for it is written,* 'He will give His angels charge concerning You to guard You,' and 'On their hands they will bear You up, Lest You strike Your foot against a stone.' "[29]

Jesus still clung to the Scriptures as a buffer against the onslaught of the devil. "Jesus said to him, 'On the other hand, *it is written,* "You shall not tempt the Lord your God." ' "[30]

After the temptations, Jesus "returned to Galilee in the power of the Spirit."[31] He went to Nazareth where He had been brought up. As was His custom, He went to the synagogue on the sabbath.

> The book of the prophet Isaiah was handed to Him. And He opened the book, and *found the place where it was written,*
> The Spirit of the Lord is upon Me,
> Because He anointed Me to preach the gospel to the poor.
> He has sent Me to proclaim release to the captives,
> And recovery of sight to the blind,
> To set free those who are downtrodden,
> To proclaim the favorable year of the Lord.' "[32]

Jesus had a special message to give to His family and hometown friends. He found the exact place in the Scriptures that told of His global mission. He found the one that applied to His own good news.

The Sermon on the Mount proffered by Jesus was almost completely elaborated from the Old Testament Scriptures. In the fifth, sixth, and seventh chapters of Matthew we find references from Exodus, Leviticus, Numbers, Deuteronomy, Kings, Job, Psalms, Proverbs, Ecclesiastes, Isaiah, Jeremiah, and Hosea.[33]

When the Pharisees criticized Jesus for eating with tax collectors and sinners, He recited a passage from the prophet Hosea: "But go and learn what this means, 'I DESIRE COMPASSION AND NOT SACRIFICE, for I did not come to call the righteous, but sinners.' "[34]

Another time Jesus cautioned His disciples that the time would come when they would be taken prisoners. He assured them through the words of the Book of Samuel that the Spirit of God would give them the right thing to say.

> When they deliver you up, do not become anxious about how or what you will speak; for it shall be given you in that hour what you are to speak. For it is not you who speak, but it is the Spirit of your Father who speaks in you.[35]

John the Baptist was having second thoughts about whether Jesus was really the promised Messiah. He was sitting in prison examining all that he had seen and heard. Jesus sent a message to John taken from the Old Testament prophecy of Isaiah:

> The BLIND RECEIVE SIGHT and the lame walk, the lepers are cleansed and the deaf hear, and the dead are raised up, and the POOR HAVE THE GOSPEL PREACHED to them.[36]

John's messengers returned to John with the message from Jesus, and Jesus turned to the crowd to talk about John. He drew on passages from the Book of Malachi: "This is the one about whom it is written,/'Behold, I send My messenger before Your face,/who will prepare Your way before You.' "[37]

One of Jesus' most beautiful invitations had its corresponding verse in the Book of Jeremiah:

> Come to Me, all who are weary and heavy-laden, and I will give you rest. Take My yoke upon you, and learn from Me, for I am gentle and humble in heart; and YOU SHALL FIND REST FOR YOUR SOULS. For My yoke is easy, and My load is light.[38]

Jesus was criticized when His disciples ate grain on a sabbath as they were walking through the grain fields. Jesus reminded His critics of the story of David who ate the holy bread when he was running from his enemies:

> Have you not read what David did, when he became hungry, he and his companions; how he entered the house of God, and they ate the consecrated bread, which was not lawful for him to eat, nor for those with him, but for the priests alone?[39]

Jesus was popular for the parables He taught. He had a reason for speaking in parables—one that He quoted to His disciples from the Book of Jeremiah: "Therefore I speak to them in parables; because while seeing they do not see, and while hearing they do not hear, nor do they understand."[40] Then Jesus continued with a passage from

Isaiah: "In their case the prophecy of Isaiah is being fulfilled, which says, 'You will keep on hearing, But you will not understand.' "[41]

Jesus often referred to famous personages of the Scriptures:

I say to you, that many shall come from east and west, and recline at the table with *Abraham,* and *Isaac,* and *Jacob,* in the kingdom of heaven.[42]

An evil and adulterous generation seeks after a sign; and a sign will not be given it, except the sign of *Jonah.*[43]

The *Queen of the South* shall rise up with this generation at the judgment and shall condemn it, because she came from the ends of the earth to hear the wisdom of *Solomon;* and behold, something greater than Solomon is here.[44]

The scribes and the Pharisees have seated themselves in the chair of *Moses.*[45]

At other times Jesus merely referred to scriptural passages in generalized statements: "You have heard that is was said."[46] "It was also said."[47] Again you have heard that it was said to the men of old."[48] "Go and learn what this means, 'I desire mercy, and not sacrifice.' "[49] "Have you not read."[50] "It is written."[51] "Yes; have you never read."[52] "Have you not read what was said to you by God."[53]

It is no wonder that Matthew tells us:

The result was that when Jesus had finished these words, the multitudes were amazed at His teaching: for He was teaching them as one having authority, and not as their scribes.[54]

He Had a Genuine Love for People

Looking at him, Jesus felt a love for him (Mark 10:21).

Jesus believed in love—a love that was selfless, giving, forgiving, and all-inclusive. "A new commandment I give to you, that you love one another, even as I have loved you, that you also love one another."[55]

How did Jesus love the disciples? He loved them in spite of their unbelief, their bickerings, their complaining, their resentments, their nagging, their betrayal, and their denial. Jesus knew who was going to betray Him, yet He loved Judas so much that, even to the time of betrayal, no one was able to guess who the guilty one would be. Jesus loved Peter all the way through, although He knew Peter was going to deny Him. And His love followed through, even after His death, burial, and resurrection. After the resurrection, Jesus, in His concern and love for Peter, had the angel say to the women who went to the grave to anoint His body;

> Do not be amazed; you are looking for Jesus the Nazarene, who has been crucified. He had risen; He is not here; behold, here is the place where they laid Him. But go, tell His disciples and Peter, He is going before you into Galilee.[56]

What a show of special love for the one who chided Him, reproved Him, argued with Him, and denied Him! This is the kind of love that Jesus wanted His disciples throughout the ages to practice. Love— forgiving, making allowances for, understanding love.

A young man came to Jesus seeking eternal life. Jesus talked with him for a while and saw his sincerity, his intensity, and his reasoning. He also saw the fallacy in his thinking and his overcoming weakness. But the Scriptures tell us that in spite of all this, "Jesus looking upon him loved him."[57]

Jesus did not have to condition Himself to love. He *was* love! It flowed out of Him to others: young and old, rich and poor, bad and good. His great love! His all emcompassing love! His love freely given!

What kind of love did Jesus have? He had ABIDING LOVE: "Just as the Father has loved Me, I have also loved you; abide in My love."[58]

He gave His disciples the secret of abiding in His love: "If you keep My commandments, you will abide in My love; just as I have kept My Father's commandments, and abide in His love."[59]

Jesus' love was *unending:*

Now before the Feast of the Passover, Jesus knowing that His hour had come that He should depart out of this world to the Father, *having loved His own who were in the world, He loved them to the end.*[60]

Jesus' love was *sacrificial:* "Greater love has no one than this, *that one lay down his life for his friends. You are My friends,* if you do what I command you."[61]

When Jesus spoke these words He knew that He was going to die for these self-asserting disciples as well as the self-interest seeking crowds. Paul spoke of Jesus' sacrificial love: "Walk in love, just as Christ also loved you, and gave Himself up for us, an offering and a sacrifice to God as a fragrant aroma."[62]

John caught the spirit of Christ's love: "We know love by this, that He laid down His life for us; and we ought to lay down our lives for the brethren."[63]

Jesus' love is *all-inclusive:* "For God so loved the world, that He gave His only begotten Son, that *whoever believes* in Him should not perish, but have eternal life."[64]

Jesus' love is *unconditional:* "In this is love, not that we loved God, but that He loved us and sent His Son to be the propitiation for our sins. Beloved, if God so loved us, we also ought to love one another. . . . We love, because He first loved us."[65]

Jesus' love is *beyond understanding:* "To know the love of Christ which surpasses knowledge."[66]

Jesus' love is GOD'S LOVE: "Beloved, let us love one another, for love is from God; and every one who loves is born of God and knows God.[67]

There was nothing false or pretended about Jesus' love. His love was so sincere that He was willing to cancel His personal plans and change the direction of His work in order to meet the needs of those who were clamoring for His attention.

He Was More Concerned with "Interior Decorating" than "Exterior Decorating"

Out of the heart. (Matt. 15:19).

Jesus was never overconcerned about reputation. He never emphasized "making a good impression." He never told His disciples to keep up a "good image" or to project a "positive image." He was more interested in the actual character of a person. Many times we read that He spoke of the inner person and the value of correcting any basic weaknesses.

> For the mouth speaks out of that which fills the heart. The good man out of his good treasure brings forth what is good; and the evil man out of his evil treasure brings forth what is evil.[68]

> The things that proceed out of the mouth come from the heart, and those defile the man. "For out of the heart come evil thoughts, murders, adulteries, fornications, thefts, false witness, slanders. These are the things which defile the man."[69]

Jesus praised many characteristics that carnal mankind despises. His Beatitudes equate these traits with happiness and joy. They were strengths, not weaknesses. The Beautitudes dealt with a person's interior:

> Happy are those who know they are spiritually poor; . . .
> Happy are those who mourn . . .
> Happy are those who are humble; . . .
> Happy are those whose greatest desire is to do what God requires;
> Happy are those who are merciful to others; . . .
> Happy are the pure in heart.[70]

I feel sure that Jesus knew well the story of Samuel. He went to anoint a replacement for Saul, Israel's first king. Samuel was told by God:

> Do not look at his appearance or at the height of his stature, because

I have rejected him; for God sees not as man sees, for man looks at the outward appearance, but the Lord looks at the heart.[70]

Jesus condemned wrong heart attitudes:

You have heard that it was said, "You shall not commit adultery"; but I say to you, that everyone who looks on a woman to lust for her has committed adultery with her already in his heart.[72]

Jesus said to them, "You are the ones who make yourselves look right in other people's sight, but God knows your hearts. For the things that are considered of great value by man are worth nothing in God's sight."[73]

Jesus warned His hearers about working to improve only the outward appearance:

Woe to you, teachers of the law and Pharisees, you hypocrites! You clean the outside of the cup and dish, but inside they are full of greed and self-indulgence. Blind Pharisees! First clean the inside of the cup and dish, and then the outside also will be clean.[74]

Through consistent prayer and Scripture study, Jesus managed to keep the inside of His "cup" clean, so His outward words and actions were always in accord with the will of God, His Father.

Notes

1. Matthew 5:48
2. Matthew 26:29, RSV
3. Luke 2:49, KJV
4. Luke 12:32
5. John 5:43
6. John 14:2
7. John 15:10
8. John 12:49
9. Matthew 11:27
10. John 5:17
11. John 5:19-20; 5:26; 20:21; 5:30; 10:30; 14:31, GNB, 15:9
12. John 17:4, 6-10; 16:28
13. Hebrews 5:7-8
14. John 10:27-30, RSV; Matthew 18:19; John 5:24; 6:37-40; John 14:13; 15:7; 15:16; 16:23b-24
15. Isaiah 40:31
16. Mark 1:35-37; Luke 5:15-16; Matt 14:23

98

17. Matt. 26:36; 11:25; 14:19

18. Luke 6:12

19. Luke 9:18

20. Matthew 6:7-9 (author's italics)

21. Matthew 6:6 (author's italics)

22. Mark 11:24 (author's italics); Luke 18:1,7-8

23. Luke 11:9-10, 13

24. Luke 2:41-45

25. Luke 2:46

26. Luke 4:1

27. Luke 4:4 (author's italics)

28. Luke 4:8 (author's italics)

29. Luke 4:9-11 (author's italics)

30. Matthew 4:7 (author's italics)

31. Luke 4:14

32. Luke 4:17-19 (author's italics)

33. Exodus 20:4; Leviticus 19:12: Numbers 30:2; Deuteronomy 24:1-4, 2 Kings 4:33; Job 38:41; Proverbs 25:8; Ecclesiastes 5:2 Isaiah 66:1

34. Matthew 9:13; Hosea 6:6

35. Matthew 10:19-20; 2 Samuel 23:2

36. Matthew 11:5; Isaiah 35:4-6

37. Matthew 11:10; Malachi 3:1

38. Matthew 11:28-29

39. Matthew 12:3

40. Matthew 13:13; Jeremiah 5:21

41. Matthew 13:14-15; Isaiah 6:9-10

42. Matthew 8:11 (author's italics)

43. Matthew 16:4 (author's italics)

44. Matthew 12:42 (author's italics)

45. Matthew 23:2 (author's italics); 17:11; 23:35; 24:15

46. Matthew 5:27, 38, 43

47. Matthew 5:31, RSV

48. Matthew 5:33, RSV

49. Matthew 9:13 RSV; Hosea 6:6

50. Matthew 19:4, RSV

51. Matthew 21:13, RSV

52. Matthew 21:16d, RSV

53. Matthew 22:31, RSV

54. Matthew 7:28

55. John 13:34

56. Mark 16:6-7

57. Mark 10:21, RSV

58. John 15:9

59. John 15:10

60. John 13:1 (author's italics)

61. John 15:13 (author's italics)

62. Ephesians 5:2

63. 1 John 3:16

64. John 3:16 (author's italics)

65. 1 John 4:10-11, 19

66. Ephesians 3:19

67. 1 John 4:7

68. Matthew 12:34b-35

69. Matthew 15:18-19; Mark 7:20-23; Matthew 23:27-28; 5:20

70. Matthew 5:1-8, GNB

71. 1 Samuel 16:7

72. Matthew 5:27-28; 15:7-8; John 7:24

73. Luke 16:15, GNB

74. Matthew 23:25, NIV; 23:23; 7:21-22

13

What Motivated Jesus

Therefore you are to be perfect, as your heavenly Father is perfect.
(Matt 5:48).

How often we read in the Old Testament Scriptures: "Speak to all the congregation of the sons of Israel and say to them, 'You shall be holy, for I the Lord your God am holy.' "[1]

This was God's ancient charge to the Jewish people. Jesus not only took this standard for His own life, but He taught it to His disciples: "Therefore you are to be perfect, as your heavenly Father is perfect."[2]

After Jesus returned to heaven, Peter would write in one of his Epistles: "Like the Holy One who called you, be holy yourselves also in all your behavior; because it is written, 'You shall be holy, for I am holy.' "[3]

Jesus became what God wanted Him to be. He became the love of God, the mercy of God, the righteousness of God, and the glory of God! He never forgot *who* He was: the Son of God. He resided in the Father, He obeyed His commandments, He walked in His light, and He kept communication lines open by constant contact with the Father. He never made a major decision without first consulting His Lord. He never forgot His "land of loyalty"—heaven. He always remembered His mission and let nothing deter Him in His march toward His goal.

Jesus did not hide Himself in a sanctuary to escape problems, responsibilities, and tribulations. He moved out into the mainstream of life with the masses of people. He lived with the people, identified with them, and at the same time kept Himself unspotted by the sins of the people. He did not let their sins make Him less an example of "God on earth." Although the disciples and bystanders provoked Him to exasperation, He controlled His inner being which made it possible for Him to control His environment.

Jesus wasn't impressed by wealth or people of influence. He was touched by the needs and sufferings of the lowly and humble and those who were reaching for the same ideal. He believed: "You shall love the Lord your God with all your heart, and with all your soul, and with all your mind, and with all your strength."[4] He said: "My food is to do the will of Him who sent Me, and to accomplish His work."[5] "I am not looking for human praise."[6]

Jesus was not cocky or overly self-confident: "I can do nothing on My own initiative."[7]

These were strange words for a man who knew He was the Son of God. He did not declare Himself as a "self-made man." Even being the Son of God did not give Him, at the time of His presence here on earth, the confidence and authority to do His "own thing" under His own power. He had no feeling of "self-importance" because more than once He said, "I do not seek My own will, but the will of Him who sent me."[8]

He Had a Purpose

My Father, . . . Thy will be done (Matt. 26:42).

The cause and purpose of Jesus were intertwined. His cause was the salvation of human souls. The purpose of His life was to do the will of His Father: be the Messiah. "For even the Son of Man did not come to be served but to serve, and to give His life a ransom for many."[9]

It was the will of God that Jesus should sacrifice Himself for the sins of the world.

Toward the end of His life, in agonizing prayer, Jesus stated the basic reason for His life:

"You are a king, then!" said Pilate. Jesus answered, "You are right in saying I am a king. In fact, for this reason I was born, and for this I came into the world, to testify to the truth."[10]

Now my soul has become troubled; and what shall I say, "Father, save Me from this hour"? But for this purpose I came to this hour. "Father, glorify Thy name."[11]

I have come to bring fire to the earth, and, oh, that my task were completed! There is a terrible baptism ahead of me, and how I am pent up until it is accomplished![12]

Satan tried by all means to abort Jesus' mission before He reached the cross. Satan attacked Him with heavy trials and problems that would have deterred even the strongest of men; he threatened Jesus' life with premature death; he hounded Him with discouragement, ridicule, and disbelief. Jesus was literally fighting for His life—to protect it in its entirety, so He could arrive at the cross and *give* it for humanity's redemption.

Although He was committed to the will of God, Jesus hoped His Heavenly Father would find an alternative to the cross:

Horror and dismay came over him, and he said to them, "My heart is ready to break with grief; stop here, and stay awake." Then he went forward a little, threw himself on the ground, and prayed that, if it were possible, this hour might pass him by. "Abba, Father," he said, 'all things are possible to thee; take this cup away from me. *Yet not what I will, but what thou wilt.*' "[13]

He went away a second time, and prayed: "My Father, if it is not possible for this cup to pass me by without my drinking it, *thy will be done.*" . . . So he left them and went away again; and he prayed the third time, using the same words as before.[14]

Conformity to the will of God was His purpose, but it was the hardest thing He was ever called upon to do.

For I have come down from heaven not to do my will but to do the will of him who sent me. And this is the will of him who sent me, that I shall lose none of all that he has given me, but raise them up at the

last day. For my Father's will is that everyone who looks to the Son
and believes in him shall have eternal life.[15]

He Had a Cause

I lay down My life for the sheep (John 10:15).

The Son of Man has come to seek and to save that which was lost.[16]

Jesus was the Son of man. In His own words He explained the
reason for His sojourn here on earth.

I lay down My life for the sheep. And I have other sheep, which are not
of this fold; I must bring them also, and they shall hear My voice; and
they shall become one flock with one shepherd. For this reason the
Father loves Me, because *I lay down My life that I may take it
again.*[17]

From the time of the original sin of Adam and Eve, God had
promised a Messiah, a Savior of mankind to restore persons to communion with God. Speaking to the serpent, the perpetrator of the
original sin, God said:

And I will put enmity
Between you and the woman,
And between your seed and her seed;
He shall bruise you on the head,
And you shall bruise him on the heel.[18]

Through the years of the formation and purification of the Jewish
nation, the promise of a Savior/Messiah was before the people. To the
first patriarch God promised: "In your seed all the nations of the earth
shall be blessed, because you have obeyed My voice."[19] Through
Jacob, grandson of Abraham, came the continued promise:

Judah, your brothers shall praise you;
....
The scepter shall not depart from Judah,
until he comes to whom it belongs.[20]

Through Moses, the liberator, we have this word:

> The Lord your God will raise up for you a prophet like me from among you, from your countrymen, you shall listen to him. . . . And the Lord said to me, "They have spoken well. *I will raise up a prophet from among their countrymen like you, and I will put My words in his mouth, and he shall speak to them all that I command him."*[21]

Then the prophecies became more frequent and more specific:

> I will surely tell of the decree of the Lord:
> He said to Me, "Thou art My Son,
> Today I have begotten Thee.
> Ask of Me, and I will surely
> give the nations as Thine inheritance,
> And the very ends of the earth as Thy possession."[22]

> Therefore the Lord Himself will give you a sign: Behold, a virgin will be with child and bear a son, and she will call His name Immanuel.[23]

> For a child will be born to us,
> a son will be given to us;
> And the government will rest
> on His shoulders;
> And His name will be called Wonderful Counselor, Mighty God,
> Eternal Father, Prince of Peace.
> There will be no end to the increase
> of His government or of peace.[24]

The fifty-third chapter of Isaiah portrays the life and cause of the promised Messiah. The prophets Jeremiah, Micah, Zechariah, Haggai, and Malachi all pointed to the coming Messiah. The Jewish people lived in expectancy—the Messiah might come at anytime!

And He did come: Jesus of Nazareth, Son of God! He did not come as a privileged prince in a palace, but as an humble, common man, subject to temptations, problems, trials, and tribulations. Why did He do this?

Since then the children share in flesh and blood, He Himself likewise also partook of the same, that through death He might render powerless him who had the power of death, that is, the devil; and might deliver those who through fear of death were subject to slavery all their lives.[25]

"Even the Son of Man did not come to be served, but to serve, and to give His life a ransom for many."[26]

Jesus had a cause! He was the only One in all God's eternity that was able to cleanse the sins of God's human creation and bring them back into oneness with God. The problems, temptations, and tribulations of Jesus here on earth were harsh, bitter, and almost unbearable.

In his life on earth Jesus made his prayers and requests with loud cries and tears to God, who could save him from death. Because he was humble and devoted, God heard him. But even though he was God's Son, he learned through his sufferings to be obedient. When he was made perfect, he became the source of eternal salvation for all those who obey him.[27]

Jesus' dedication to the cause of the salvation of human souls was so great He was able to overcome the major and minor problems of this life, knowing that the greatest problem of all was still to be faced. He had to keep His eyes fixed on that one cause, putting all else behind Him. He pressed on toward the one big cause of His life.

Now is my soul troubled; and what shall I say? Father, save me from this hour: but for this cause came I unto this hour.[28]

I am speaking of the bread that comes down from heaven, which a man may eat, and never die. I am that living bread which has come down from heaven; if anyone eats this bread he shall live for ever. Moreover, the bread which I will give is my own flesh; I give it for the life of the world.[29]

He Got His Priorities
in Order

Seek first His kingdom and His righteousness (Matt. 6:33).

Once Jesus chose His ideal, discovered the purpose for His life, and found the cause for which He had been born, the priorities and meaning of His life fell into a natural pattern.

The temporal things of this world immediately took a back seat. He wasn't concerned about having a home: "Jesus said to him, 'The foxes have holes, and the birds of the air have nests; but the Son of Man has nowhere to lay His head.' "[30] He wasn't worried about what clothes He should wear or where He would get them; He wasn't concerned about what He would eat or where the food would come from or if He would have enough:

> For this reason I say to you, do not be anxious for your life, as to what you shall eat, or what you shall drink; nor for your body, as to what you shall put on. Is not life more than food, and the body than clothing? Look at the birds of the air, that they do not sow, neither do they reap, nor gather into barns, and yet your heavenly Father feeds them. Are you not worth much more than they? . . . And why are you anxious about clothing? Observe how the lilies of the field grow; they do not toil nor do they spin, yet I say to you that even Solomon in all his glory did not clothe himself like one of these. . . . Do not be anxious then, saying "What shall we eat?" or "What shall we drink?" or "With what shall we clothe ourselves?" . . . for your heavenly Father knows that you need all these things.[31]

The disciples once went into the village of Sychar to obtain food. Since Jesus was tired He waited at the well outside of town. When the disciples came back they were "begging Jesus, 'Teacher, have something to eat!' But he answered, 'I have food to eat that you know nothing about.' "[32]

And you remember what happened when Jesus was in the wilderness after His baptism:

After fasting forty days and nights, he was hungry. The tempter came
to him and said, "If you are the Son of God, tell these stones to become
bread." Jesus answered, "It is written: 'Man does not live on bread
alone, but on every word that comes from the mouth of God.' "[33]

What was Jesus' attitude about material things?

Do not be afraid, little flock, for your Father has been pleased to give
you the kingdom. Sell your possessions and give to the poor. Provide
purses for yourselves that will not wear out, a treasure in heaven that
will not be exhausted, where no thief comes near and no moth destroys.
For where your treasure is, there your heart will be also.

Jesus' priorities all centered around the eternal and the spiritual. He
was always seeking out the will of His Heavenly Father. He spent His
leisure and private hours in prayer. He was based in the Scriptures.
Whenever He was in a synagogue, He knew where to find the passages
He needed for His lessons. Wherever He was on the sabbath, He
sought out a synagogue.

Jesus worked hard at keeping His attitudes and aspirations based
on His relationship with God, His Father, "because I always do what
pleases him."[35]

My Father has never yet ceased his work, and I am working too.
. . . In truth, in very truth I tell you, the Son can do nothing by himself;
he does only what he sees the Father doing: what the Father does, the
Son does. For the Father loves the Son and shows him all his works.[36]

Jesus set a pattern and an example for all posterity:

For to this you have been called, because Christ also suffered for you,
leaving you an example, that you should follow in his steps. He committed *no sin; no guile* was found on his lips. When he was reviled, he *did
not revile* in return; when he suffered, he *did not threaten;* but he trusted
to him who judges justly. He himself bore our sins in his body on the
tree, that we might die to sin and live to righteousness. *By his wounds
you have been healed.*[37]

Notes

1. Leviticus 19:2
2. Matthew 5:48
3. 1 Peter 1:15-16
4. Mark 12:30
5. John 4:34
6. John 5:41, GNB
7. John 5:30*a*
8. John 5:30*b*
9. Mark 10:45
10. John 18:37, NIV
11. John 12:27
12. Luke 12:49, TLB
13. Mark 14:33-36, NEB (author's italics)
14. Matthew 26:42-44, NEB
15. John 6:38-40, NIV
16. Luke 19:10, NIV
17. John 10:15*b*-17 (author's italics)
18. Genesis 3:15
19. Genesis 22:18
20. Genesis 49:8*a*-10*a*, RSV (author's italics)
21. Deuteronomy 18:15,17-18 (author's italics)
22. Psalms 2:7; 45:2
23. Isaiah 7:14
24. Isaiah 9:6; 11:10; 28:16
25. Hebrews 2:14-5, 17-18
26. Mark 10:45
27. Hebrews 5:7-9, GNB
28. John 12:27, KJV
29. John 6:50-51, NEB
30. Matthew 8:20
31. Matthew 6:25-33
32. John 4:31-32, GNB
33. Matthew 4:2-4, NIV
34. Luke 12:32-34, NIV
35. John 8:29, GNB
36. John 5:17*b*-20, NEB
37. 1 Peter 2:21-24, RSV (author's italics)

14

The Paradox of Winning and Losing

Can any good thing come out of Nazareth? (John 1:46).

His parents were from a small, insignificant town up country. A popular saying was: "Can anything good come out of Nazareth?"[1] When He was presented in the Temple, His parents were so poor they could give only the cheapest sacrifice required.[2] It could be assumed that His parents were not as careful about His welfare as they should have been because on one occasion they lost Him for three days.[3]

His stepfather, Joseph, was a carpenter who trained Him in this profession,[4] but probably His father died while He was young and He, being the oldest,[5] had full responsibility for the family.

When He was thirty years old,[6] He left home, sought out a popular evangelist, and was baptized publicly. He then became an evangelist and traveled extensively in His home country. Most of His chosen helpers were from the lower social class. He was poor all of His life. He didn't own a home, He borrowed boats for crossing the sea, and ate whenever and wherever He could, sometimes going hungry.

According to worldly standards He was a natural "born loser."

But when He started preaching, teaching, healing, and working miracles, His career took an upsurge. He had crowds following Him day and night. They listened to Him and marveled. They were not only impressed by what He said but the way He said it. Once the crowds wanted to make Him a king. Another time the people had a procession for Him and crowded around shouting: "Hosanna! Blessed is he who comes in the name of the Lord! Blessed is the kingdom of our father David that is coming! Hosanna in the highest!"[7]

He merited the confidence of His followers to the extent that they asserted, "If he has to die, let us go to Jerusalem and die with him;" And "Even if all the world deserts you, you can count on me."

He became so well known that the people in all the surrounding cities and areas heard about Him. He was known by the religious and political leaders of the day.[8] The multitudes about Him were so vast that He couldn't even go into the cities and was forced to stay in the open places out in the country.

Although jealousy and envy caused His death, even there He was honored. Over the cross where the poor carpenter was crucified there hung a sign in three languages that said: JESUS OF NAZARETH, THE KING OF THE JEWS.[9] He was buried in the tomb of one of the wealthiest men in town, a respected member of the council. At the tomb, the government placed soldiers (an honor guard?) to keep watch.

Yes! This man who had such humble beginnings became a winner, even in His death. Aren't His disciples known throughout the world today? And hasn't the course of history been changed because of His life, death, and resurrection? Modern history dates from His lifetime. Through His death He won eternal life for all His disciples. He was seen returning to heaven (from which He originally came), and is expected to return at any time.

> I go to prepare a place for you. And if I go and prepare a place for you, I will come again, and receive you to Myself; that where I am, there you may be also . . . I will not leave you as orphans; I will come to you.[10]
>
> In the world you have tribulation, but take courage; I have overcome the world.[11]

Can a Born Winner Lose?

Where is He who has been born King of the Jews? (Matt. 2:2).

Although Jesus came from a poor home, his parents had every reason to expect success for Him. His birth was predicted to both parents beforehand. An angel choir sang the announcement of His birth. Wise Men from the East came to adore Him with costly gifts of gold, frankincense, and myrrh. He was circumcised at the proper time and dedicated according to the law of Moses, redeeming Him as the firstborn son.

He was brought up in a small, but busy town where He learned an honest trade taught by Joseph. He was the oldest of several children and learned responsibility early. He was taken to the Temple when He was twelve. He was so intelligent and wise He was able to carry on long discussions with learned doctors of the Law. He had a sense of mission at an early age, for didn't He say to His parents: "Did you not know that I must be in my Father's house?"[12] Each day "Jesus kept increasing in wisdom and stature, and in favor with God and men."[13]

When a well-known evangelist came through the country Jesus was already an established young man. He went to one of the meetings and accepted baptism, making known His personal dedication to God.

He left His business and started traveling around the country, preaching. We know He was popular because He was always surrounded by crowds. He was socially aware because He gave away free food, made the sick well, and worked other miracles. He loved the poor and little children. He was kind and courteous to women.

He was honored at dinners, almost always had high officials in attendance at His discourses, was anointed with expensive perfume, given a seamless robe, and had a whole fishing fleet at His disposal. He had the power to produce food and used His power to minister to huge crowds. He was honored in a parade and had a committee of women that ministered to His well-being.

He had all the makings of becoming a popularly elected "Savior/ King"—carried to success by the "will of the people."

But somewhere along the way a few people began to sense that things were not going too well. He was criticized, rebuked, attacked, and threatened with assassination. His own family became concerned about His sanity. The religious leaders openly attacked Him. His loyalty to the government was questioned. He did not fit into the mold made for the "promised Messiah" by the common people and religious leaders of that day. He was outspoken against popular traditions and contemporary thought. He was very rigid in His demands about little things like attitudes, intentions, and methods of accomplishing things. He didn't give proper reverence to the religious leaders. He began to give time to foreigners, outcasts, and beggars. He associated with the wrong crowd.

It seems that His brilliant career was headed for complete disaster. People began to desert His group. Even members of His inner council began to have arguments about job classification. One of them sold out to the opposition.

He became pessimistic and began to predict an early death for Himself.

In the end, He was arrested by an armed guard (accompanied by a mob) and tried in court. He was sentenced to be crucified with two criminals. The crowds who followed Him in the beginning and hailed Him as king later on were the very same ones that demanded His crucifixion. Even on the cross He was ridiculed, mocked, and jeered. Only a few of His closest friends went to His crucifixion: the rest of them abandoned Him when the "showdown" came. Apparently, He was a loser.

But . . .

Although He *lost* the crowds,

He *lost* part of His family,

He *lost* the battle with the Pharisees and the Sadducees, and

He *lost His life;*

He won:

Approval from His Heavenly Father

Salvation for the sinners of the world,

Loyalty from many women, relatives, and disciples.

Victory over death and the grave,

Eternity with the Father for those who have faith in Him, and

Rest from the burdens and problems of this world.

Jesus—All Alone

My God, My God, why hast Thou forsaken Me? (Mark 15:34).

Yes, we have our lovely mental images of Jesus walking along the shore of a lake with His disciples—everything calm and serene. And we tend to forget that most of the time Jesus walked among the multitudes—people pushing and shoving, trying to get closer to Him to be healed, to hear better, or just to touch Him. So many people surrounded Him that at times they threatened to crush Him.

We have our beautiful pictures of Jesus sitting calmly with little children crowding closely around. In reality, the little children, dirty, grimy, and restless, were thrust upon Him with such force and vigor that the disciples became irritated and started chiding the mothers.

Yes, Jesus was invited into fine homes and honored, but the homes were invaded by "spies" and antagonistic persons. Most of the time the dinners turned into debates, subtle digs, insults, and sometimes outright attacks.

We envision Jesus calmly strolling through the countryside. We neglect to also see Him pushing ahead, trying to reach a certain destination. We don't think of Him with the dust, the sweat, the heat, and the fatigue. We see Him taking time to teach the multitudes. When the people leave to rest, there is Jesus, surrounded by His disciples asking questions: "What did You mean by that remark?"

"Why do You teach in parables?" "Why can't we do what You do?" "Explain that lesson to us again." "I don't understand!"

We see Jesus quietly praying on the hillside, forgetting that it is midnight or the early hours of the morning—the time when the disciples and the crowds are refreshing their bodies with sleep. And even when He is in communion with His Father, the people search Him out and try to take Him back to the work.

Do you think about Jesus going home occasionally to see His relatives—His brothers, sisters, and mother, talking to His friends and neighbors? Have we forgotten that once He began His public ministry, Jesus became persona non grata in His home and hometown? He was accused of being mentally sick, being a show-off, and being irreverent. He wasn't even wanted in town. They tried to kill Him. He didn't have a home to which He could go.

Jesus loved by everybody: Isn't that what we often think? But the Pharisees and Sadducees, although bitter enemies, united in their hatred of Him. The crowds wanted something from Him, but not many even took the time to say thank you. Even His close friends, the disciple didn't understand Him—resented Him at times, complained, wanted to know "what's in it for me," and didn't pay too close attention to what He was trying to get across to them.

How could a human being (even a divinely human being like Jesus) survive the pressures, the lack of privacy, the tensions, the constant crowds, and the ever-present sense of urgency?

Jesus wrestled with the idea of the crucifixion. Should He go through with it? Did His Father have an alternative plan? Was there any other possible way to secure salvation for lost human souls? He had examined all the possibilities that His divine/human mind possessed. Up to the very last moment He was searching for an escape that was within the permissive will of His Father.

He went a little beyond them, and fell on His face and prayed, saying, "My Father, if it is possible, let this cup pass from Me; yet not as I will, but as Thou wilt."[14]

Even up to the last hour Jesus could have called twelve legions of angels: the thought must have come to Him many times during the hours of agony and humiliation. Even on the cross it was not too late to call down help from God His Father.

But there *did* come an hour when the act was irreversible. The awfulness of the sins of the world weighed heavily upon Him to the point of excruciating pain. He could think on only one recourse—He would call upon His Father. His Father was the only One He had ever been able to trust, to turn to, to commune with. The weight of the sins of the whole world crushed His soul and His spirit. It was then that Jesus faced the greatest tribulation and trial of His life. He turned His eyes and His heart heavenward and called to His Father.

All through His earthly ministry He had treasured His growing awareness of the power and presence of His Heavenly Father. Jesus foresaw the cross and abandonment by His disciples. He had told them:

Behold, an hour is coming, and has already come, for you to be scattered, each to his own home, and to leave Me alone; and yet I am not alone, because the Father is with me.[15]

Did Jesus not foresee the time when His Father, who is Holy God, would have to turn His face away because He could not look on the awful sin that Jesus was bearing?

He Was Alone—All Alone! "My God, My God, why hast Thou forsaken Me?"[16]

The plan of salvation was conceived in heaven. God was the Author. When Jesus came to earth and was revealed as God's Son, they worked together—God the Father and God the Son. But there was one time in all eternity when frail humanity had to walk alone—those last moments on the cross! God could not look on His Son. He turned His face. Jesus Was All Alone. Oh, the desolation!

How we praise His name that we will never have to come to this point. Through Jesus' supreme sacrifice of being completely isolated from the Father with the sins of the world upon Him, He built a bridge that forever links us with the heavenly realms. "No, never alone" we sing with grateful hearts.

Never again will anyone need to be so completely alone. Jesus' example through real-life experiences here on earth, His accomplishments against overwhelming odds, His confidence and victory over all kinds of problems in all types of situations have made Him more than just the Savior of our souls. He is our shining, victorious Example. He is the Lord of our lives. He has shown the way. He has walked the roads before us. He has won the battle over everyday nagging and persistent problems. But more, He has promised that we, too, can follow His example, for we can walk in His steps with His personal help and Presence:

> He Himself has said, "I will never desert you, nor will I ever forsake you.[17]
>
> The one who comes to Me I will certainly not cast out.[18]
>
> Come to Me, all who are weary and heavy-laden, and I will give you rest. Take My yoke upon you, and learn from Me, for I am gentle and humble in heart; and YOU SHALL FIND REST FOR YOUR SOULS. For My yoke is easy, and My load is light.[19]
>
> I will not leave you as orphans; I will come to you.[20]
>
> With God all things are possible.[21]
>
> You call Me Teacher and Lord; and you are right; for so I am.[22]
>
> Whatever you ask in My name, that will I do, that the Father may be glorified in the Son. If you ask Me anything in My name, I will do it.[23]
>
> Peace I leave with you; My peace I give to you; not as the world gives, do I give to you. Let not your heart be troubled, nor let it be fearful.[24]

> In the world you have tribulation, but take courage; I have overcome the world.[25]

Jesus could have chosen an easier way. He could have ingratiated Himself with the religious leaders who came to hear and question; He could have planned His program around Jewish tradition and practice; He could have succumbed to the charms of the many women who surrounded Him night and day; He could have couched religious truths in an elaborate vocabulary to appeal to the elite and educated minority; He could have dressed His teachings in humor; and He could have dismissed the argumentative, contentious, and disrespectful disciples.

He *could* have done all these things and many more, but He *didn't*. Jesus had an option. He did not have to obey His Heavenly Father; He was not obligated to use the Father's plan. He could have insisted on using His own ideas and methods. But He *didn't*. Jesus *chose* to follow the Father's plan for His life down to the minute details, and He left us the challenge: "I gave you an example that you also should do as I did to you."[26]

Peter told us: "For to this you have been called because Christ also suffered for you, leaving you an example, that you should follow in his steps."[27]

Notes

1. John 1:46, RSV
2. Luke 2:24; Leviticus 12:8
3. Luke 2:42-46
4. Mark 6:3
5. Mark 6:3
6. Luke 3:23
7. Mark 11:9, RSV
8. Matthew 14:1
9. John 19:19
10. John 14:2*b*-3, 18
11. John 16:33*c*
12. Luke 2:49, RSV
13. Luke 2:52
14. Matthew 26:39
15. John 16:32-33
16. Matthew 27:46*b*
17. Hebrews 13:5
18. John 6:37

19. Matthew 11:28-29
20. John 14:18
21. Matthew 19:26
22. John 13:13
23. John 14:13-14
24. John 14:27
25. John 16:33c
26. John 13:15
27. 1 Peter 2:21, RSV

15

Postscript: A Remembrance of Humanity from the Divine

Do you love Me? (John 21:15).

Peter was restless and depressed. He couldn't quieten his spirit. He couldn't put all the pieces together—the walk with Jesus, His death and resurrection, and the future. Most of all, Peter couldn't accept his own behavior in the face of all the circumstances. He was the one who had followed from the very first. He was one of the three chosen to be with Jesus at the transfiguration, the healing of Jarius's daughter, and in the inner garden. He was the one who had said, "You are the Christ, the Son of the living God," when Jesus asked, "Who do you say that I am?"[1] But HE was also the one who said, "Even though all may fall away because of You, I will never fall away"[2] when Jesus talked about being abandoned. He was the one who had denied his Lord Jesus—not just once, nor twice, but three times. He was the one who was so scared that the last time he denied Jesus he even resorted to the "old ways" and emphasized his denial with profanity and an oath.

Abruptly, Peter stood to his feet and exclaimed, "I am going fishing."[4] Six of the other disciples who were there with him, sensing his mood, stood with him and said, "We will also come with you."

It was a trying night. Professional fishermen, some of them, and they caught nothing!! "Let's go in," someone said, and they began pulling for the shore. It was getting light by now. A man was standing on the shore. "Have you caught anything?" He shouted. "Nothing," came back the reply from the boat.

118

"Throw the net out to starboard, friends, and you will find something." They looked at each other and shrugged their shoulders. Maybe He could see something from shore that they couldn't see. They picked up the net and dropped it over the side. Suddenly, there were so many fish that they could not pull the net into the boat.

"It is the Lord!" exclaimed the disciple that Jesus loved.

At the words *It is the Lord,* Peter, who had practically nothing on, wrapped his cloak around him and jumped into the water. The other disciples came on in the boat, towing the net and the fish.

Jesus had prepared breakfast for His beloved companions: bread and charcoal-broiled fish. How good it smelled! Peter didn't know what to say. He shifted from one foot to the other, and Jesus said, "Bring some of the fish you have now caught." Peter gratefully turned around, rushed back to the boat, went aboard, and helped drag the net to shore. So many! One hundred and fifty-three big ones!

"Come and have breakfast," Jesus said. They rubbed their hands together and walked over to where the food was waiting. Jesus stepped forward and served them bread and fish, as He had done on other occasions.

Peter kept looking at Jesus as he ate. What was He thinking? What was going to happen next? What a strange place for Him to meet them. How did He know where they would be? But, of course, He was the Messiah! Jesus spoke softly, "Simon, son of John, do you love Me more than these?" Peter caught his breath. (Why did He ask *him* that question? Why did He single him out? What did He mean by "more than these?" Was Jesus referring to Peter's rash affirmation that *he* would not fall away even if all the other disciples did? Was He thinking about Peter's bold brag that he would even die with Him rather than deny Him?) "Yes, Lord; You know I love You."

Jesus looked keenly at Peter. (This was his chance to clear his conscience. This was the opportunity he had asked for to obtain forgiveness.)

"Feed My lambs," said Jesus.

Peter looked at his feet. He scuffed the ground with his toes. He could not bring himself to look into Jesus' eyes. Everyone was looking at him: he sensed their stares.

"Simon, son of John," (Peter looked into the eyes of Jesus,) "do you love Me?" (Not "more than these," just "do you love Me?")

Peter replied much too quickly, "Yes, Lord; You know that I love You." (Peter rebuked himself silently, *why* couldn't he throw himself before Jesus' feet and say, "Lord, forgive me, I'm sorry that I denied You. I'm sorry I ran away. I'm sorry I didn't believe You and rush up to Galilee to meet You after the crucifixion. Forgive me, Lord. *I do love You!*")

Jesus looked lovingly at Peter. How He wanted to help him. "Shepherd My sheep."

Peter's spirit fell within him. He dropped his eyes again,

"Simon, son of John,"—there, that name again. (Why was He using the name that went back to Peter's fishing days, before he knew Jesus? Was Jesus trying to humiliate him—to embarass him before the other disciples? Was Jesus "getting even with him" by asking him the same question *three times* just because he had denied Jesus three times?) "Do you love Me?" This time Jesus' voice was clear and sharp.

Peter exploded, "Lord, You know all things; You know that I love You."

Jesus sadly shook His head. He had given Peter a chance to ask for forgiveness, a chance to regain his exuberance, his self-confidence, his freedom from guilt, and his pardon. But Peter responded only halfway. Jesus said to him, "Tend My sheep."[5]

Peter was agitated. He turned the attention from himself. He looked at John, whom Jesus loved. "What about him, Lord?" There—the moment had passed, and Jesus' attention was turned to another.

Jesus had tried to help one of His disciples win over a personal problem. But this time pride had won out.

The Irony of It All

On the Lamb were wounds that once had caused his death (Rev. 5:6 *b*, TLB).

For God took the sinless Christ and poured into him our sins. Then, in exchange, he poured God's goodness into us! (2 Cor. 5:21, TLB).

We can be sure that we do not stand in an unknown world when we have problems. There is Someone who knows everything about problems, Someone who confronted them all victoriously without sin—Jesus of Nazareth, now Jesus Christ, the Son of God. He walked on the same earth we walk on with the same problems. When we go to Him with our problems, He can identify.

He left us His life, His example, and His methods as a pattern for facing and overcoming problems. We can go to Him personally and talk to Him about our problems. We can ask for His help and be assured that He will guide and direct us to a solution. It may not come as an instantaneous answer; it may delay days, weeks, months, or even years. But the answer *will* come. God's timing is never wrong. We can be confident that in God's time there will be a proper response from Him.

We need to remember that problems are a necessary way of life. They are the means by which we are cleansed, refined, and perfected. James told us to count it all joy "when [we] meet various trials." The reason? "For you know that the testing of your faith produces steadfastness."[6]

Peter told us:

In this you rejoice, though now for a little while you may have to suffer various trials, *so that the genuineness of your faith,* more precious than gold which though perishable is tested by fire, *may redound to praise and glory and honor* at the revelation of Jesus Christ.[7]

He also encouraged us with these words,

After you have suffered a little while, the God of all grace, who has called you to his eternal glory in Christ, will himself restore, establish, and strengthen you.[8]

We have this admonition:

Humble yourselves therefore under the mighty hand of God, that in due time he may exalt you. Cast all your anxieties on him, for he cares about you.[9]

Let us get ready for the problems and temptations. Let us be prepared for the battles that we know are coming. We don't know how they will come or what their nature will be, but we can know with a certainty that they WILL appear. Paul told us *how* to prepare:

Finally, be strong in the Lord and in the strength of his might. Put on the whole armor of God, that you may be able to stand against the wiles of the devil. . . . Stand therefore, having girded your loins with *truth,* and having put on the breastplate of *righteousness,* and having shod your feet with the equipment of the *gospel of peace;* besides all these, taking the shield of *faith,* . . . And take the helmet of *salvation,* and the sword of the Spirit, which is the *word of God.*[10]

Let us live a joyful, victorious Christian life—not in spite of—but because of our problems. Let's learn to "Rejoice always, pray constantly, give thanks in all circumstances; for this is the will of God in Christ Jesus for you."[11]

For to this you have been called, because Christ also suffered for you, leaving you an example, that you should follow in his steps. He committed no sin; no guile was found on his lips. When he was reviled, he did not revile in return; when he suffered, he did not threaten; but he trusted to him who judges justly. He himself bore our sins in his body on the tree, that we might die to sin and live to righteousness. By his wounds you have been healed."[12]

How incredible it is to think that *Jesus,* who faced all temptations and problems known to persons without sinning at any time, is the only One in the new "world to come" who will not be spotless. He will bear the scars of the very sin to which He did not succumb, while we, who are there, bought by the blood of His righteousness, will be spotless and devoid of all marks of sin—cleansed by the blood of the Lamb of God.

> For our sake he made him to be sin who knew no sin, so that in him we might become the righteousness of God.[13]

> Having been made perfect, He became to all those who obey Him the source of eternal salvation.[14]

> It was fitting that we should have such a high priest, holy, innocent, undefiled, separated from sinners and exalted above the heavens.[15]

> It was fitting for Him, for whom are all things, and through whom are all things, in bringing many sons to glory, to perfect the author of their salvation through sufferings.[16]

> Consider Him who has endured such hostility by sinners against Himself, so that you may not grow weary and lose heart.[17]

> Since He Himself was tempted in that which He has suffered, He is able to come to the aid of those who are tempted.[18]

> Jesus Christ is the same yesterday and today, yes and forever.[19]

> Worthy art thou to take the scroll and to open its seals,/for thou wast slain and by thy blood didst ransom men for God/from every tribe and tongue and people and nation.[20]
> Worthy is the Lamb who was slain, to receive power and wealth and wisdom and might and honor and glory and blessing! . . . To him who sits upon the throne and to the Lamb be blessing and honor and glory and might for ever and ever! . . . Amen![21]

Notes

1. Matthew 16:15-16, RSV
2. Matthew 26:33
3. Matthew 26:72-74

4. John 21:3-12
5. John 21:15-17
6. James 1:2-3, RSV

7. 1 Peter 1:6, RSV (author's italics)

8. 1 Peter 5:10, RSV

9. 1 Peter 5:6-7, RSV

10. Ephesians 6:10-17, RSV (author's italics)

11. 1 Thessalonians 5:18, RSV

12. 1 Peter 2:21-24, RSV

13. 1 Corinthians 5:21, RSV

14. Hebrews 5:9

15. Hebrews 7:26

16. Hebrews 2:10

17. Hebrews 12:3

18. Hebrews 2:18

19. Hebrews 13:8

20. Revelation 5:9, RSV

21. Revelation 5:13-14, RSV